The Aging Well Workbook For Anxiety And Depression

CBT Skills To Help You Think Flexibly And Make The Most Of Life At Any Age

Julie Erickson, PhD
Neil A. Rector, PhD

16pt

Read How You Want

LARGE PRINT BOOKS, BRAILLE & DAISY

Copyright Page from the Original Book

NEW HARBINGER PUBLICATIONS is a registered trademark of New Harbinger Publications, Inc.

New Harbinger Publications is an employee-owned company.

Copyright © 2023 by Julie Erickson and Neil A. Rector
New Harbinger Publications, Inc.
5720 Shattuck Avenue
Oakland, CA 94609
www.newharbinger.com
All Rights Reserved

Cover design by Amy Daniel; Acquired by Georgia Kolis; Edited by Elizabeth Dougherty

---

Library of Congress Cataloging-in-Publication Data on file

TABLE OF CONTENTS

"The *Aging Well Workbook for Anxiety and Depression* is an essential guide for older adults looking to improve their mental health. Written by a mental health expert, this practical workbook provides effective strategies and exercises to manage anxiety and depression in a clear and concise way. It's a must-read for anyone who wants to age well and maintain their mental well-being."

—**Eric Lenze, MD,** Renard professor; and head of psychiatry at Washington University School of Medicine in St. Louis, MO

"*The Aging Well Workbook for Anxiety and Depression* is a terrific and much-needed addition to the field. Cognitive behavior therapy (CBT) has all too often been treated as a one-size-fits-all-ages approach. Julie Erickson and Neil Rector ably zoom in on the concerns of older adults, and provide clear, concrete recommendations for dealing with the challenges of later life."

—**Randy J. Paterson, PhD, RPsych,** author of *The Assertiveness Workbook* and *How to Be Miserable*

"*The Aging Well Workbook for Anxiety and Depression* is a lovely resource for older adults who experience anxiety and/or depression, and their providers and families. Educational background material and skills to manage anxiety and depression are clearly described and solidly

rooted in scholarly evidence. Case examples and practice exercises integrated throughout the workbook add to its clarity and relevance. An excellent addition to the self-help literature."
—**Melinda A. Stanley, PhD,** distinguished emeritus professor of psychiatry at Baylor College of Medicine, board member of the TLC Foundation for Body-Focused Repetitive Behaviors, and coauthor of *Abnormal Psychology*

"Aging not only brings physical ailments, but can also come with anxiety and depression. Fortunately, there are relatively easy and effective methods to target these problems. Julie Erickson and Neil Rector's *The Aging Well Workbook for Anxiety and Depression* describe these methods and guide you through them. I highly recommend this book."
—**Stefan G. Hofmann, PhD,** Alexander von Humboldt professor at Philipps University of Marburg in Germany

"This new book by Erickson and Rector is an outstanding resource for anyone who wants to learn about using CBT for the management of anxiety and depression in later life. It is easy to read, and the authors have provided excellent case examples, tables, and figures to illustrate concepts that are important to understand in the management of anxiety and depression in later life using CBT."

—**Rajesh Tampi, MD, MS, DFAPA, DFAAGP,** professor, chairman, and Bhatia Family Endowed Chair in the department of psychiatry at Creighton University School of Medicine

"With their unique insights into the research and life experiences of older adults, Erickson and Rector provide clear, practical, step-by-step instruction on how to use the most effective tools of CBT to overcome anxiety and depression. Their numerous case examples illustrate how to tailor specific CBT strategies to the problems and challenges of aging. The workbook offers a positive, hopeful outlook, becoming an essential resource for any seniors not experiencing the golden years of life."

—**David A. Clark, PhD,** professor emeritus at the University of New Brunswick; and author of *The Anxious Thoughts Workbook, The Negative Thoughts Workbook,* and *The Anxious Thoughts Workbook for Teens*

"If you're an older adult and find you're worried or down much of the time (or you care about an older person who's anxious or down), then you need this wonderful workbook. Depression and anxiety aren't the norm, even when older adults have health problems or other life difficulties. This easy-to-read manual will teach you invaluable skills for improving your mood, getting back into the swing of life, and achieving your goals."

—**Judith Beck, PhD,** president of The Beck Institute for Cognitive Behavior Therapy, and author of books for consumers on using CBT for weight loss and maintenance

For DE and SE

For NDG, DCF, and DJR

Foreword

The *Aging Well Workbook for Anxiety and Depression* by Julie Erickson and Neil Rector is a much-needed resource for the millions of people and their families coping with the difficulties that may arise from aging. Ironically, almost all published research in psychology is based on college students between 18 and 22, with very little on the important segment of the population that is the elderly. Indeed, there is scarcity of professionals who are trained in gerontology, and this will become even more obvious as the population continues to age.

Two recent books help us understand how the aging process can be either a difficult one or a positive one, depending on how we are prepared for it and how we respond to it. For example, a recent book by Arthur Brooks, *From Strength to Strength,* illustrates the importance of being realistic about the changes that may occur in one's professional functioning as one ages and of having the willingness and flexibility to embrace the next stage in life—particularly with the knowledge that it might be one of greater wisdom and a wider perspective on what is important and what is of value. Brooks notes the importance, as we age, of personal relationships—both intimate relationships and friendships—and of the sense of purpose and valued activity that one has in life. He also notes that being able to pivot from previous roles that one had a younger age to different roles as one gets older is an adaptive strategy. Another recent book that is particularly relevant is *The Good Life: Lessons from the World's Longest Scientific Study of Happiness* by Robert Waldinger and Marc Schulz. This book documents a longitudinal study that began at Harvard and South Boston in the 1930s and continues to the present day. In it, Waldinger and Schulz interviewed young men and women and followed them through their lifetime to answer a question: what is associated with psychological well-being and a longer lifespan? Again, this classic study illustrates the importance of relationships and having meaning in life. Passivity and isolation were predictors of lower psychological well-being and higher mortality rates.

The Aging Well Workbook for Anxiety and Depression is an excellent application of the main principles of cognitive behavioral therapy (CBT) to the issues that arise for elderly people. For many people, as they get older, there may be a resignation to loss of energy, loss of roles, and loss of some relationships, which further adds to the risk of depression and anxiety. However, Erickson and Rector correctly indicate that this resignation does not have to be the inevitable response to aging. In fact, biases about the elderly are not supported by the facts. For example, depression is not the most common experience for those who are elderly; depression and anxiety, ironically, are higher for people between the ages of 18 and 25. We live in an ageist society that privileges youth and appearance to the detriment of elderly people, who unfortunately are often viewed as useless, past their prime, or a burden to others. But in reality, only a small percentage of elderly people have significant disability or dementia. Most are not depressed, and many have excellent intimate relationships and friendships.

Ultimately, as the population ages, we need to address the issues that elderly people do face. Fortunately, the data indicate that elderly people respond as well as younger people to CBT. Each chapter in this highly practical book describes the main CBT approaches that are relevant to anxiety and depression in the elderly. There are clear examples, forms to complete for self-assessment, and helpful guides to reversing the negative thinking, passivity, and isolation that characterize depression and anxiety at any age. One can even argue that some of the unique challenges that the elderly may face—such as illness, loss of a loved one, loss of occupational or relationship roles, and loss of some abilities such as hearing—necessitate a CBT toolbox to help them modify biased negative thinking, passivity, and isolation and adopt a flexible problem-solving approach to life. The same processes that have been identified as helpful for anxiety and depression are also directly relevant to helping the elderly.

The ultimate message here is that what matters is how you cope with the onset of aging. To give you an example, a lawyer friend who is 77 decided that he wanted to learn some new skills in his 70s. He took guitar lessons, learned Italian (while translating Dante's *Inferno)*, and even learned to swim. He is now working on writing a book on history. He has a wonderful relationship with his wife of ten years and his mood is as good as one could wish. He has used a proactive, engaging, behaviorally active approach that has enriched his life. And, as another friend once told me, "It's never too late to have a second childhood."

—Robert L. Leahy, PhD

Author of *If Only.... Finding Freedom from Regret*

Introduction

If you're reading this book, there's a good chance you're struggling. Perhaps you've had one too many sleepless nights because you're worrying. Or maybe your spouse has raised concern about how down you've been recently. You may even be worrying *about* your worrying and how quickly this can compound and impact your life. If you're dealing with mental health difficulties, you know how quickly and easily they can compound and make you feel like you're struggling to stay afloat. Like many older adults, you may not know where and how to get help for issues with anxiety or depression. You might feel uncomfortable talking to others about your difficulties let alone talk to a therapist. You might even doubt *if* you can feel better.

You're not alone. As many as 15 percent of adults over the age of sixty can struggle with some form of anxiety or mood disorder (Reynolds et al. 2015). Although the prevalence of most mental disorders tends to decrease as people get older, the burden of anxiety and depression can be just as heavy. Untreated difficulties with anxiety and depression can greatly reduce your quality of life and make it difficult to enjoy many of the things that are a part of growing older. The so-called golden years can be far from golden when you're dealing with relentless anxiety or debilitating depression.

The good news is, there is hope. Cognitive behavioral therapy (CBT) is considered the gold standard of psychological treatment for a wide variety of mental health difficulties, including anxiety disorders and depression. It is an evidence-based treatment, meaning that decades of scientific research support its effectiveness in treating mental health difficulties across the life span. There is considerable evidence suggesting that is helpful for treating mental health conditions experienced by older adults, such as anxiety disorders and depression (Gould et al. 2012a; Gould et al. 2012b).

Not only is CBT effective, but its benefits are maintained over time. In many research studies, people who have had CBT treatment have shown to maintain improvements for up to several years (DiMauro et al. 2013; Wiles et al. 2016). That's rather remarkable when you consider that most courses of CBT treatment occur over ten to fourteen weeks. Plus, there's more good news. It turns out that CBT can be just as effective as medication treatment for anxiety or depression (Roshanaei-Moghaddam et al. 2011). Which is great for older adults who don't want to add yet another medication to their pill organizer. We told you there was hope.

As much as CBT is an effective and efficient treatment modality for older adults, not everyone has access to this form of treatment. Mental health professionals who specialize in geriatric psychology or psychiatry can be in short supply.

This is expected to get only worse as the Baby Boomer generation of adults gets older and demand for these services increases. Depending on where you live and your personal circumstances, psychological treatment may be cost prohibitive or inaccessible. Further, some older adults may feel embarrassed or ashamed to go therapy. Stigma around seeking mental health services still exists, unfortunately.

It was for these very reasons that this book came to be. We recognized that older adults are a neglected and underserved population with respect to mental health services and CBT in particular. Older adults tend to seek psychological treatment at lower rates relative to other age groups (Mackenzie, Pagura, & Sareen 2010). There are also very few self-help resources that are written with the needs of older adults in mind. Late adulthood can be a time of many changes such as retirement, becoming a grandparent, physical health challenges, and changes in mobility among many other things. Older adults experience cognitive and emotional changes that make this stage of life unique relative to other age groups. Additionally, for older adults who struggle with anxiety or mood disorders, they may report different symptoms than younger adults do and benefit from alterations to treatment (Erickson & Rector 2022; Christensen et al. 1999). As such, older adults should have self-help resources that reflect an understanding of this unique time in life and how mental health difficulties are experienced and treated in late life.

As clinical psychologists who work routinely with older adults and have practiced, taught, and studied CBT for more than forty years collectively, we recognized a pressing need for this book. Our older clients have long voiced the need for a book written specifically for them, reflecting the fact that many of the existing CBT workbooks don't speak to the needs and issues experienced by older adults. Our goal was to write a comprehensive and practical CBT self-help workbook specifically for older adults—the first of its kind. It's important to know that this book is not intended to be a substitute for group or individual CBT with a mental health care provider. Rather, it is a self-guided resource that older adults with anxiety and depression can work through to learn better strategies for coping with their difficulties (did we mention that the strategies that are backed by decades of scientific research?).

We hope that what you learn in this book not only helps you better manage any feelings of anxiety or depression that you may be experiencing but also ultimately helps you better the quality of your life. Late adulthood can be an incredibly satisfying and fulfilling time in life. Many of the developmental tasks of early to mid-adulthood, such as raising children and career advancement, are complete or less time consuming. For some, there can be more freedom from certain responsibilities or obligations and more time to pursue interests and hobbies. Older adults can possess greater knowledge and understanding of themselves along with the wisdom and maturity accumulated from a lifetime of experiences. While aging is often stereotypically painted as a depressing time, the reality can be the exact opposite.

That being said, late adulthood can also be a time of significant change, transition, and loss. Physically, you might experience more aches and pains, and chronic or acute health issues. You may have reduced mobility, be less able to do certain tasks, and require more help from others. Relationships with adult children can be difficult to manage, strained, or nonexistent. Losing a significant other can be devastating and leave you feeling directionless and not like yourself. Transitioning from a career to retirement can come with a loss of identity and difficulties finding purpose. All of these changes can be very challenging emotionally, physically, and socially. Navigating the peaks and valleys of late life requires a certain degree of adaptation and flexibility (but thankfully not the physical kind). Our hope is that this book help you cultivate just that and situates you make your latter years the best that they possibly can be.

WHAT TO EXPECT

This book contains ten chapters, each covering a different concept or strategy designed to help you better manage your anxiety or depression. We'll begin with an introduction to CBT to help you have a better understanding of its history and what this approach is all about. As part of chapter 1, we'll answer common questions that people have about CBT. Chapters 2 and 3 will give you the ins and outs of anxiety and depression—what they are, when they might be considered normal, when they would be considered a disorder, and what some of most common anxiety and depressive disorders are. We'll speak specifically to how difficulties with anxiety and depression can present in older adults versus younger adults. As part of these chapters, you'll complete a self-assessment of symptoms to help flag areas of difficulty.

Chapters 4 and 5 cover two important CBT fundamentals: goal-setting and self-monitoring. Setting goals may seem like a no-brainer, but we'll discuss why this is so important and some of the common mistakes people make in doing this. By setting goals, you'll identify what areas of your life you want to change, which will help direct your efforts for applying CBT strategies. Self-monitoring refers to identifying your thoughts, behaviors, emotions, and physical sensations. Although this sounds straightforward, it can be surprisingly difficult to know the differences between them and be able to name what they are. We'll talk about each in more detail and help you learn how to identify your emotions, thoughts, behaviors, and physical sensations. Being able to distinguish these features will help you apply the strategies covered in chapters 6 and 7.

Changing our patterns of thinking is an important skill that can help alter our emotional reactions and behavioral responses, which you'll read about in chapter 6. Altering problematic behaviors that maintain anxiety and depression, such as avoidance or overdoing, is covered in detail in chapter 7. As part of this chapter, you'll be exploring how facing your fears and reengaging in mood-boosting activities can help reduce anxiety and depression and increase the quality of your life.

In chapter 8, we shift into discussing problem-solving, which can often be a challenge to do when dealing with anxiety or depression. As you grow older, there's no shortage of problems that require finding and implementing solutions. Acknowledging that there are some situations that cannot be changed despite our best efforts, we move into discussing acceptance in chapter 9. In chapter 10, we talk about how to prevent future relapses and maintain the progress you've made while working through the book.

To set reasonable expectations, this book will by no means be a cure-all. When people are looking to make improvements in their mental health, it often requires a variety of different supports, resources, and time. You can count on this book being a useful tool to add to your tool kit of strategies and resources.

HOW TO BENEFIT FROM THIS BOOK

This book is meant to be consumed slowly and thoughtfully. Take your time as you read each chapter to ensure that you are grasping the material and have an opportunity to apply it your own life. You might consider doing one chapter a week to allow you sufficient time to read and process the content and complete the exercises within each chapter. It can be helpful to make your own notes as you read the book or highlight passages that resonate with you. If you struggle with any form of cognitive impairment, in addition to writing your own notes as you read each chapter, you may want to talk out loud and summarize your understanding of the chapters.

There are exercises to complete both within and at the end of each chapter to help you apply what you are reading to your own life. (Blank forms for many of the exercises can be found at http://www.newharbinger.com/51260.) While it might be tempting to skip these exercises, it's no understatement to say that they are the most important sections of the book. Completing these exercises will ultimately help you learn new ways to respond to your thoughts and feelings and reduce behaviors that keep you stuck feeling anxious or depressed. Practice doesn't make perfect, but it does help us change.

Lastly, as you read this book, you may be reflecting on how significant others in your life may be impacted by or play a role in your difficulties with anxiety or depression. It may be beneficial to share part of what you're learning in this book with trusted people in your life. In doing so, they may better understand your difficulties and your efforts to change and how they may be of help. Telling others about what you've learned in this book is also another way to solidify your own understanding of the material.

This book is not meant to replace CBT treatment done with a therapist but may be used in conjunction with such work. If you are looking to find a CBT therapist to help you with your difficulties, you may wish to speak with your family doctor or consult online resources, such as the Association for Behavioral and Cognitive Therapies, to locate someone near you.

We hope you find this book to be useful, rewarding, and helpful in shifting your perspective and experience of growing older. The writer and activist Betty Friedan once said, "Aging is not 'lost youth' but a new stage of opportunity and strength." We couldn't agree more.

PART I

Understanding CBT and the Nature of Anxiety and Depression in Later Life

CHAPTER I

All About Cognitive Behavioral Therapy

- *Cognitive behavioral therapy (CBT) was created by Aaron Beck and is considered the leading, evidence-based psychological treatment for a wide variety of mental health difficulties.*
- *CBT centers around the idea that thoughts, behaviors, emotions, and physical sensations are interrelated.*
- *The goal of CBT is to make changes in how you think and behave in order to alleviate emotional and physical distress and better your quality of life—and it works.*

There's no better way to get you started on your journey to improve your mental health later in life than getting to know the approach we'll use to get there: cognitive behavioral therapy (CBT). This chapter is designed to give you a thorough introduction to CBT, including what this approach is, where it originated, and its underlying conceptual model. By understanding this approach in more detail, you'll be better able to appreciate its relevance and usefulness to you. You'll be examining your own experiences from a CBT perspective and in doing so, see the connection between your emotions, thoughts, behaviors, and physical sensations. We will also review some common questions people have about CBT, especially older adults participating in this form of treatment. You'll finish this chapter with a solid grasp of this approach and greater clarity about how it will help you deal with anxiety or depression.

WHAT IS CBT?

So, what the exactly is cognitive behavioral therapy (CBT)? Nearly sixty years old, CBT is one of the leading forms of psychological treatment worldwide. It is an approach backed by decades of scientific research and is widely recognized and respected by mental health professionals. It is among the most common treatment modalities taught in training programs for mental health professionals.

There are a number of ways in which CBT treatment differs from other forms of psychotherapy. One is its emphasis on short-term treatment. CBT doesn't occur over years but over a matter of weeks. If you are working with a CBT therapist, your length of treatment can range from approximately eight to fourteen sessions, depending on the reason you're seeking treatment and the severity of your difficulties. That's great news for anyone who doesn't want to spend years in therapy.

Second, CBT is goal directed, meaning that anyone participating in this form of therapy is encouraged to identify what they want out of treatment and what their goals are. That could be, for example, spending more time with friends, engaging in more physical activity, communicating more effectively with loved ones, or confronting a feared situation. CBT is focused on moving toward a point on the horizon, and you're the one who identifies that point.

Third, CBT is focused on helping clients learn new strategies and tools to help them manage their difficulties more effectively. As much as therapy can be about talking and being listened to, CBT is also focused on educating people with both a framework to understand their difficulties and a set of tools and strategies to help them cope more effectively. In a way, the goal of CBT is for you to become your own CBT therapist. You should walk away from treatment having a good understanding of the CBT model and an array of tools in your tool kit for dealing with your issues.

A fourth way in which CBT is different from other psychotherapies is its emphasis on what is maintaining problems as opposed to exploring the root causes of problems. This means it is focused more on interrupting and changing thoughts and behavioral patterns in the present, as opposed to analyzing and understanding the origins and causes of those patterns. We don't always need to know where certain behaviors or thoughts came from in order to change them, which can be freeing.

Finally, CBT places considerable emphasis on doing homework outside of treatment sessions to help practice and implement what you're learning. This could include, for example, writing out your thoughts, feelings, and behavior in a given situation; facing a feared scenario; or engaging in a mood-boosting activity. Like most new skills, they take practice to become more habitual. When older adults engage in CBT, many of them have been thinking and behaving in particular ways for *decades*, which means it's important to be patient with yourself as you learn and try to implement new ways of coping. Let's delve a little deeper into the origins of CBT and some important underlying concepts.

CBT was developed nearly sixty years ago by Aaron Beck, a psychiatrist from the University of Pennsylvania. The treatment was quite different from other forms of psychotherapy at the time.

The prevailing form of treatment, psychoanalytic therapy, focused on the role of our unconscious minds and childhood experiences in causing psychological problems. This treatment was typically long term (we're talking years) and required a substantial investment of time and energy to sometimes unclear benefit. Beck was investigating psychoanalytic therapy with depressed patients and was surprised when his findings countered its fundamental premises. He noticed that the thoughts his patients voiced in the moment were often quite negative and seemed to have a strong impact on their mood. These thoughts were seemingly automatic. As Beck helped patients identify these automatic thoughts, he also tried to help them evaluate their thinking and look for more realistic interpretations. In doing so, patients started feeling better emotionally and engaged more in their lives. It donned on Beck that thoughts, emotions, and behaviors were interconnected. And voilà, CBT was born.

The underlying rationale of CBT can be summarized by a relatively simple diagram, shown in figure 1.

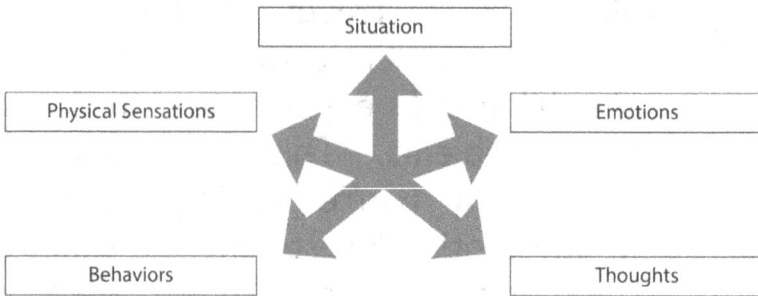

Figure 1. Diagram of underlying rationale of CBT.

The situations we encounter in daily life give rise to emotions, thoughts, behaviors, and physical sensations. Emotions can usually be identified in one word and include, for example, sadness, anxiety, guilt, shame, anger, disgust, surprise, or delight. Thoughts are the verbal statements inside our head that often occur automatically (for example, *What if I don't have enough money to retire?* or *Why am I having this hip pain?*). Behaviors are the observable actions we take, or sometimes don't take (for example, going for a walk or avoiding a phone call). Physical sensations can accompany or trigger emotions and include, for example, increased heart rate, muscle tension, or lethargy.

DID YOU KNOW...

Aaron Beck passed away in 2021 at the age of 100. He was publishing and contributing to the field even up until his death.

None of these exist in a vacuum, however. Our thoughts, feelings, behaviors, and physical sensations affect one another and often in very important ways. First, our emotions impact how we think and vice versa. If you're feeling anxious or scared, you're probably more likely to worry and think about worst-case scenarios. If you're down or depressed, you will be more likely to interpret what happens to you in a negative fashion. The more you dwell on the negatives, the worse you will feel emotionally.

Second, our thoughts and behavior impact each other. If you think you won't enjoy yourself at an upcoming family gathering, you may be less inclined to attend. However, not going could affect how you think, for example, *I should be making more of an effort with my daughter-in-law* or *I'm not as close to my family as I'd like to be.* As another example, if before going on vacation, you're worrying about all the possible things that could go wrong, you may decide to spend more time planning, preparing, and creating contingency plans for various hiccups. Despite there being value in preparation, going overboard with planning may lead you to think more about what could go wrong.

Third, our behavior impacts how we feel emotionally and vice versa. People who struggle with depression can isolate or retreat from the people and things that may help improve mood. For example, forgoing a walk outside could keep your mood low or even make it worse.

Physically, this might cause someone to feel sluggish or tired. Once you're in the habit of isolating, withdrawing, and avoiding, it can be hard to break out of that. It turns out that the idea that objects at rest stay at rest isn't just restricted to physics.

Emotionally, the costs of prolonged withdrawal, isolation, and avoidance are high, for instance, causing people to feel more depressed, anxious, lonely, and hopeless. For older adults, the physical and cognitive impacts of withdrawing, isolating, and being inactive are particularly pronounced. Older adults who are less physically, socially, and cognitively active are at higher risk of dementia (Lisko et al. 2021) and mortality (Blair & Haskell 2006; Tilvis et al. 2011). We tried, but we can't think of a more convincing reason to change your behavior. And you're taking a critical first step and dipping your toes into the CBT waters. Well done.

Let's keep learning about CBT with a more specific example of how thoughts, feelings, behavior, and physical sensations influence one another.

We all will have the unfortunate opportunity in our lifetime to have to wait for the results of medical testing. Let's imagine you are waiting on the results of blood work following several weeks of feeling more fatigued than usual. The lab results are taking longer than usual, which doesn't help your anxiety, but then you *finally* get a voicemail from your doctor's office instructing you to call the office back immediately to obtain the results of your blood work.

Your thoughts may automatically turn to some worst-case scenarios, *What if it's something life-threatening? Will it be treatable? What if I won't be able to see my grandkids grow up?* Emotionally, you may start to feel uneasy and anxious. You may even notice certain physical sensations, such as knots in your stomach or tension in your muscles. You may respond behaviorally by looking up your symptoms online to see what they could mean. Before you know it, forty-five minutes may pass with you still feeling anxious and fearful about the lab results. Talk about an uncomfortable and distressing situation to find yourself in.

Let's go back in time and imagine that after hearing the voicemail from your doctor instead of thinking about catastrophic scenarios, you have the thought *Hmm, I wonder what this could be about. I won't know until I speak to the doctor. Worrying about it won't change anything. I have been in relatively good health aside from this fatigue.* How would your emotional reaction be different? You might still feel a little anxious but likely less than if you were dwelling on catastrophic possibilities. Those butterflies in your stomach? Not as noticeable. You might be more inclined to spend forty-five minutes reading your favorite book as opposed to scouring the internet and diagnosing yourself with terminal cancer.

I know what you're thinking. *This all sounds great, but my thoughts tend to happen automatically. Even when I try to think rationally, I still feel terrible.* You're absolutely right. Thoughts and emotions can occur quickly and feel like they're not under our control. The purpose of CBT is to change our *reaction* to our automatic thoughts, emotions, behaviors, and physical sensations. By changing our reaction, we can choose patterns of thinking and behaving that help lessen our emotional suffering. CBT doesn't aim to get rid of negative emotions entirely (for reasons we'll discuss in the next few chapters), but rather, it helps us to think and behave in ways that will serve us well even when we're experiencing negative emotions. Think of CBT as a way to slow down a speeding train and in some cases, redirect it to a different destination altogether.

Ok, now it's your turn to apply the CBT model to your own life. Select an example from the last week in which you felt a negative emotion. Using the prompts in figure 2, identify the situation as well as any emotions, thoughts, and physical sensations you experienced and how you behaved. An example is provided in figure 3.

Situation
Where were you?
What was happening?
Who were you with?

Physical Sensations
What did you notice in your body?

Emotions
What were you feeling emotionally?

Behaviors
How did you respond?

Thoughts
What was going through your head at the time?

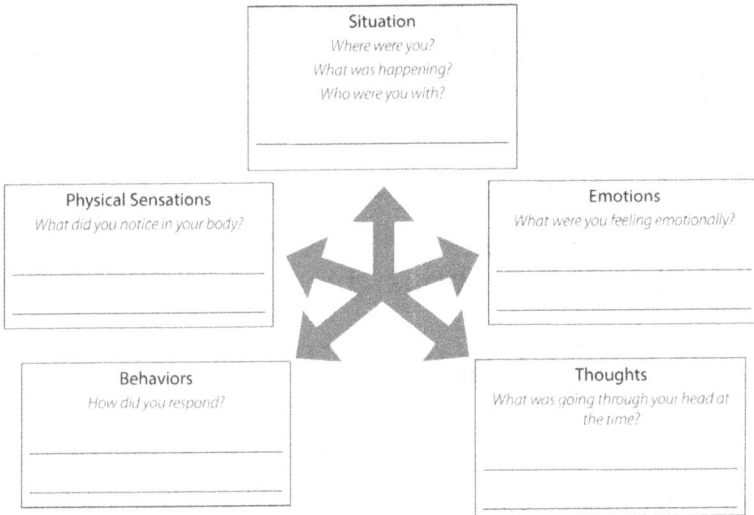

Figure 2. CBT model with prompts.

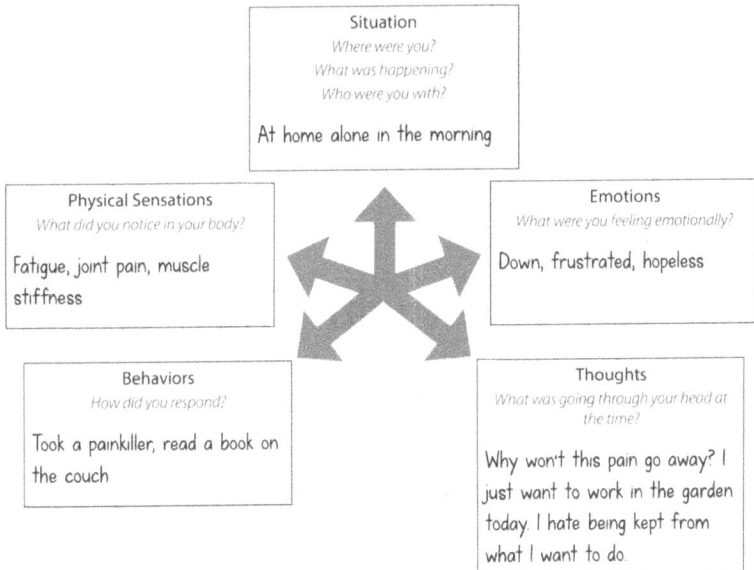

Situation
Where were you?
What was happening?
Who were you with?

At home alone in the morning

Physical Sensations
What did you notice in your body?

Fatigue, joint pain, muscle stiffness

Emotions
What were you feeling emotionally?

Down, frustrated, hopeless

Behaviors
How did you respond?

Took a painkiller, read a book on the couch

Thoughts
What was going through your head at the time?

Why won't this pain go away? I just want to work in the garden today. I hate being kept from what I want to do.

Figure 3. Example CBT model filled out.

COMMON QUESTIONS ABOUT CBT

Let's round out your initial knowledge of CBT by addressing some common questions that older adults have about this form of treatment.

What's My Role in CBT?

CBT is considered an active and collaborative psychological treatment, meaning that when as an older adult you engage in CBT, you are responsible for identifying your goals for treatment, learning the CBT model, and trying to use CBT strategies in your everyday life as often as you can. The more effort you put into CBT, the more you will benefit from it. This is especially the case while you're working through a self-help workbook.

Does CBT Work with Older Adults?

Contrary to stereotypes that older adults can be more stubborn and have a harder time changing their behavior or thoughts, a substantial body of research suggests that CBT is just as effective with older adults as it is for younger age groups (Gould et al. 2012a; Gould et al. 2012b). So, any concerns you may have about CBT being less helpful because you're an older adult are unfounded.

If Anxiety or Depression Is Not My Only Problem Can CBT Still Help?

Yes. CBT can be tailored to treat a wide range of issues, such as chronic pain, substance-use difficulties, eating disorders, grief, and relationship difficulties. All of these issues can involve experiencing negative automatic thoughts, difficult emotions, and problematic patterns of behavior. Many of the CBT interventions you'll read about in this book can be applied to a number of different types of issues. This is especially important given how common it is for people with anxiety or depression to also have other areas of concern. CBT works just as well for these individuals.

Is CBT About Learning to Think Positively?

No. Although popular belief holds that thinking positively is the cure for many maladies, this is not the goal of CBT. In CBT, we recognize that bad things happen and trying to think positively doesn't make this any less so. In fact, this can make us less prepared to deal with negative events when they happen. One of the primary goals of CBT is to help people become flexible thinkers. The emphasis is more on being realistic as opposed to being positive.

Does CBT Focus on Problems from My Childhood?

CBT tends to focus on what is maintaining problems in the present, as opposed to childhood experiences that may have caused your difficulties. Other therapy modalities, such as psychodynamic or psychoanalytic therapy, tend to focus more so on understanding early-life experiences. That's not to say that CBT doesn't focus at all on childhood. CBT examines long-standing and more deeply rooted thoughts called *core beliefs,* which may have formed in your childhood and still have an impact on you today. Examples of these beliefs include: *I'm not good enough. The world is an unsafe place. Other people can't be trusted.* We won't go into as much detail into core beliefs in this book, but many of the interventions we discuss to help change thoughts and behaviors are very much applicable and helpful for core beliefs.

I'm Cognitively Impaired. Will CBT Still Help Me?

It depends. If you have been diagnosed with a form of mild cognitive impairment, then you will likely still benefit from CBT with the use of good visual cues and memory aids to help you learn and remember content. Writing down key ideas in the form of points or saying them out loud as you read are examples of cues. Older adults with moderate to severe cognitive impairment may vary in terms of their responsiveness to CBT treatment. If in doubt, speak with your family physician, a psychiatrist, or psychologist for more help.

Is There Anyone Who Wouldn't Benefit from CBT?

Although we've highlighted how much good CBT can do for people with a wide range of issues, there may be some people who won't reap as much benefit. CBT requires some degree of self-awareness of one's thoughts, emotions, behaviors, and physical sensations. People who have limited insight into these things may find it difficult to fully benefit from CBT.

This approach also requires being willing to confront difficult emotions and the situations that can trigger them. For example, to improve anxiety in social situations, CBT encourages people to face the situations that make them feel anxious (such as going to parties, public speaking, or talking about oneself). Sometimes, people aren't ready or willing to take those steps, and understandably so. It is difficult to face these situations and the emotions that come up within them, and if you're not feeling ready for that, CBT is unlikely to be fully beneficial.

Finally, CBT tends to be more helpful for people who have some degree of confidence that they can learn new strategies and take the necessary steps to create change. You don't need to be a hundred percent certain that you can change, but some amount of openness and optimism can go a long way. If you're not there yet, then CBT may not be as effective.

When Do I Need to See a Therapist? What Is That Like?

Sometimes problems can become too much for one person to handle on their own. If your anxiety or depression is starting to significantly interfere with your social life (for example, interacting very little with other people), ability to handle everyday responsibilities (for example, making meals, paying bills, or running errands), or taking care of yourself (for example, bathing and personal grooming), then you may benefit from working with a CBT therapist individually. It is recommended that you work with a therapist who has training and experience with older adults.

When you first meet with a therapist, they'll likely spend a session or two assessing your symptoms, gathering a personal history, helping you identify for goals for therapy, and creating a specific treatment plan to meet your unique needs. CBT treatment sessions typically occur once per week for, on average, ten to fourteen weeks. Sessions are structured and usually start with setting an agenda for the meeting and briefly reviewing your week. After this, you would review any CBT homework you did from the previous week with your therapist. Subsequently, you and your therapist would talk about a specific issue you identified as important (for example, problems with sleep, communication difficulties, or lack of motivation), and your therapist would help introduce CBT strategies to assist you in dealing with this issue. Finally, you and your therapist would decide on your homework for the coming week based on what was discussed in that session. You would likely notice that working with a CBT therapist involves learning and experimenting with new strategies that will help you reach the goals you identified at the start of treatment.

Seeking help from a mental health professional is especially critical if your difficulties have become so severe that you are experiencing thoughts of suicide or self-harm. If this is the case, seek help as soon as possible from your nearest hospital or emergency department.

When Should I Consider Medication Treatment?

For some people, CBT may not be enough to reduce their problems with anxiety or depression. If your mental health difficulties are interfering with your ability to learn and implement CBT strategies, speak to your family doctor about medication treatment options. It is common for people to take medication at the same time as they are doing CBT and this can be an effective combination for older adults (Wetherell et al. 2013). Some individuals may find that being on medication helps them benefit more from CBT. One exception, however, are benzodiazepines. This is a class of drugs commonly prescribed for anxiety disorders that includes medications such as clonazepam (Rivotril), alprazolam (Xanax), and lorazepam (Ativan). These medications are fast acting and tend to relieve anxiety in the short term. In the long term, however, they can make it more difficult to learn how to cope in the absence of these medications. Further, there are more risks associated with taking benzodiazepines in later life because older adults are more sensitive to their negative side effects. If you're considering medication treatment, speak more with your doctor about the different options and their pros and cons.

TAKE-HOME POINTS

• *CBT is an evidenced-based psychological treatment that has shown to be effective for treating anxiety and depression across our life span.*

• *CBT is focused on the relationship between how you think, feel, and behave.*

• *Although we can't control our automatic thoughts, emotions, and physical sensations, CBT teaches ways to change your reaction to these internal experiences.*

PUTTING CBT INTO PRACTICE

When you find yourself in a difficult or challenging situation over the next week, complete the CBT model using the prompts in figure 4. Writing out your thoughts, emotions, behaviors, and physical sensations will help you become more aware and cognizant of how they impact one another. This is an important first step as we learn how to change our thoughts and behaviors. Figure 5 provides an example.

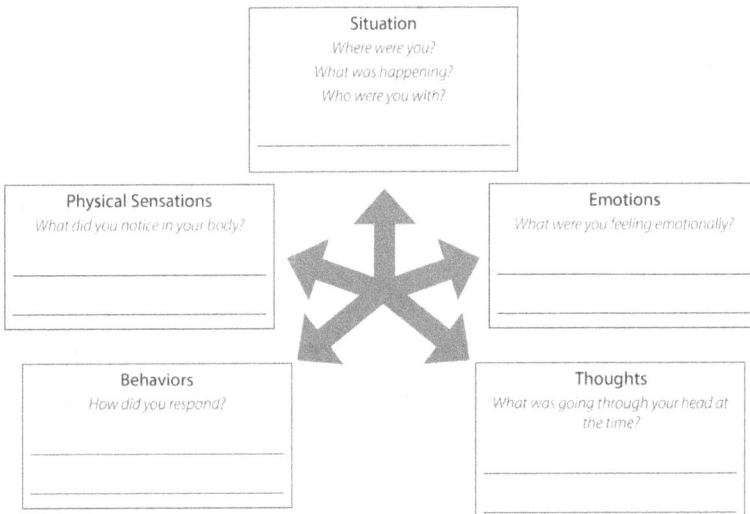

Situation
Where were you?
What was happening?
Who were you with?

Physical Sensations
What did you notice in your body?

Emotions
What were you feeling emotionally?

Behaviors
How did you respond?

Thoughts
What was going through your head at the time?

Figure 4. CBT model with prompts.

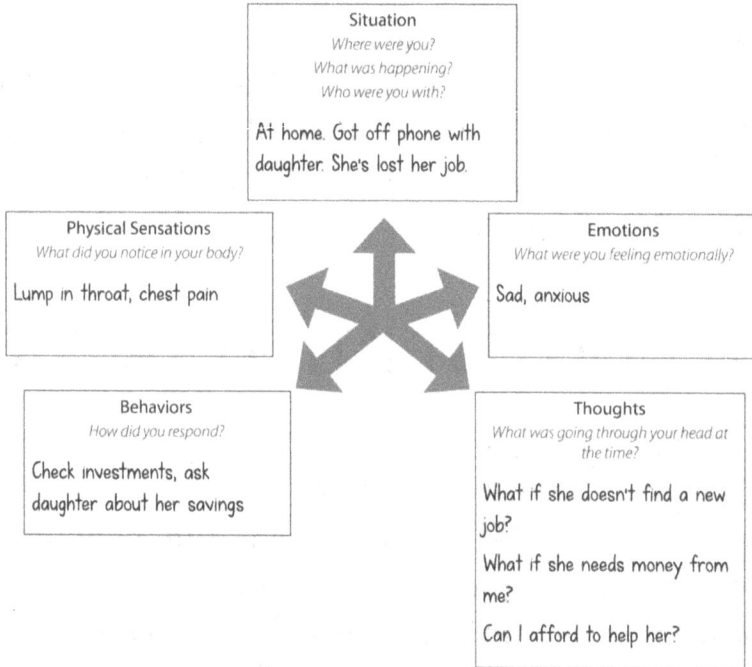

Situation
Where were you?
What was happening?
Who were you with?

At home. Got off phone with daughter. She's lost her job.

Physical Sensations
What did you notice in your body?

Lump in throat, chest pain

Emotions
What were you feeling emotionally?

Sad, anxious

Behaviors
How did you respond?

Check investments, ask daughter about her savings

Thoughts
What was going through your head at the time?

What if she doesn't find a new job?

What if she needs money from me?

Can I afford to help her?

Figure 5. Example CBT model filled out.

WHAT'S NEXT?

- *The next chapter will focus specifically on anxiety. We will define what anxiety is, why we experience it, and how it may be helpful in some cases.*
- *Keep reading to find out what constitutes an anxiety disorder, the different types of disorders, and how to help self-identify your problems.*

CHAPTER 2

Getting to Know Your Anxiety

- *Fear and anxiety are universal human emotions that have helped our species survive by activating our fight-flight-freeze response.*
- *Anxiety can start to become problematic when it's excessive for the situation, occurs more often than not, and starts to interfere with aspects of your daily life.*
- *There are different types of anxiety disorders that may be diagnosed when the problem becomes significant.*

Most older adults seeking treatment for anxiety view the emotion as a big problem, which is understandable. It can be uncomfortable and distracting, and take away from life's daily pleasures. It's safe to say that anxiety has a bad reputation. Have you ever paused to wonder why we experience anxiety in the first place? Probably not. You likely just want to get rid of it altogether. Interestingly, anxiety has had a starring role in the survival and evolution of the human species and may be more helpful than you think.

ANXIETY AND OUR BRAIN

Let us first consider our early ancestors who existed in tribes and needed to hunt and gather in order to survive. These early ancestors often found themselves in many uncertain and precarious situations as they hunted for food and resources. You might argue that trying to find a parking spot in a crowded mall during the holiday season is mighty precarious, but our early ancestors had to deal with threats of a completely different sort, including predators, inadequate food, unpredictable weather, lack of shelter or water—all with rudimentary tools and weapons. Early humans did have a very important secret weapon, however, buried deep within their brain.

Enter the *amygdala*. The amygdala is a critical part of our brain that plays an important role in memory, decision-making, and many of our emotional responses such as anger and fear. You can think of the amygdala as the brain's smoke detector. It is always on alert for the presence of danger or possible threats. When the amygdala detects a potential danger, it alerts another critical part of our brain called the *hypothalamus*. The hippocampus is responsible for orchestrating a physical response called the *fight-flight-freeze* response.

If the amygdala is the brain's smoke detector, the fight-flight-freeze response is the sprinkler system. It creates hormonal changes in our bodies that enable us to fight, run away from, or freeze in the presence of danger or threats. Increased heart rate, sweating, muscle tension, and shortness of breath (among many other sensations) are all examples of the impressively automatic responses that happen courtesy of the amygdala and hypothalamus. You may have noticed this response if you've ever narrowly avoided a car accident—your heart may race and you may be more alert to other cars immediately after this happens. This quite helpful, in fact, if it helps protect you from encountering similar types of situations in the future.

The fight-flight-freeze response enabled our early ancestors to run long distances to find food or escape predators, fight back when they were prey, or hide from a hungry bear in the woods. It's pretty impressive stuff and doesn't stop there. Not only does the amygdala have a full-time job detecting current dangers, but it also works overtime detecting *potential future* dangers. This distinction is important. Fear is the emotion that occurs in the face of current danger, whereas anxiety occurs in response to thinking about future possible dangers. For the purposes of this book, we'll focus primarily on anxiety.

In sum, fear and anxiety are two emotions with the best of intentions—they're trying to keep us safe and out of harm's way. They work in conjunction with our entire body to ensure that we respond appropriately if our survival is threatened. For the most part, they serve us very well.

So, when does anxiety start to become a problem? Here are a few ways in which this usually helpful emotion can become maladaptive:

- **Your anxiety is disproportionate to the situation.** We all worry about worst-case scenarios from time to time, but if you are preoccupied with thoughts of catastrophic worst-case scenarios that aren't likely to happen (for example, a grandchild dying while babysitting them or having a heart attack while driving), that can be one indicator that your anxiety has become a problem. It's like when your kitchen's smoke detector goes off when you've burnt toast.

- **You feel anxious most of the time.** If you feel nervous, on edge, or irritable more than half of your waking hours and can't seem to relax, you know how uncomfortable and distressing that can be. You may in turn start to feel anxious about how often you feel anxious or how little control you have over it. This can be a sign that your anxiety is a significant issue. In this case, the smoke detector won't turn off.

- **Your anxiety is interfering with important aspects of your life.** Older adults who experience significant anxiety may find that it takes away from their enjoyment of daily life or makes it more difficult to complete tasks or maintain relationships. In this case, the smoke detector makes it hard to concentrate on making dinner or talking to your spouse.

If you found yourself identifying with any of the above points, you're in the right place. Although it can be hard to recognize how much of an issue your anxiety has become and how much it has impacted your life, recognizing the problem is a critical first step toward making changes. Let's get some more practice distinguishing adaptive from maladaptive anxiety by looking at some example scenarios below. Read through each, decide whether the anxiety described is adaptive or maladaptive, and place a check mark in the appropriate box. Remember that maladaptive anxiety is disproportionate to the situation, occurs most of the time, and interferes with important aspects of life.

Adaptive Versus Maladaptive Scenarios

Scenario	Adaptive Anxiety	Maladaptive Anxiety
1. Patricia avoids going out for walks alone in her neighborhood due to fears that she might be robbed at gunpoint.		
2. Stanley feels panicked at the airport when he realizes he left his passport at home.		
3. Harpreet worries periodically about his cancer coming back in the days before follow-up appointments with his oncologist.		
4. Sharon worries nearly all the time about needing a knee replacement someday.		
5. Robert spends so much time monitoring the stock market that he's turning down social invites with friends and is losing sleep.		
6. Judy is nervous about driving on highways and plans on getting more practice during quieter times.		

Answers: 1 maladaptive, 2 adaptive, 3 adaptive, 4 maladaptive, 5 maladaptive, 6 adaptive

Now let's look at different types of anxiety problems and how they present in older adults. When anxiety difficulties get particularly maladaptive, someone may receive a diagnosis of an anxiety disorder. Mental health professionals typically use something called the *Diagnostic and Statistical Manual of Mental Disorders* (DSM) to help make diagnoses (American Psychiatric Association 2013). It's a diagnostic bible, so to speak, that identifies symptoms and determines what constitutes a mental disorder. If you are wondering how to get an anxiety disorder diagnosis, it's important to consult your family doctor, psychologist, or psychiatrist. For the purposes of this book, we'll help you identify possible areas of concern.

GENERALIZED ANXIETY DISORDER: CASE EXAMPLE

Tina is a 70-year-old, retired elementary school teacher who described herself as being a worrier for most of her adult life. She said that if she "just kept busy" she could often manage her anxiety. It wasn't until she retired three years ago that she noticed a significant increase in her anxiety. She says that she tends to worry about everything, including being on time for appointments, having enough money for retirement, and the health and well-being of her husband (who has multiple sclerosis) and three grandchildren. She thinks that much of her worry is unnecessary as many aspects of her life are going quite well. Nonetheless, Tina feels like she can't catch a break from worry and is starting to get concerned about how it's impacting her health. She can often find it challenging to relax and fall asleep and feels generally fatigued most days. Her anxiety is also making it hard to concentrate at times. She finds it challenging to engage in hobbies that she used to, such as oil painting and reading, because her mind feels distracted by worry. Tina's husband has started to express concern about her and encouraged her to talk to their family doctor about treatment options.

As you can see from Tina's experience, generalized anxiety disorder (GAD) involves having worries about a number of different areas of one's life. It can involve thinking about worst-case scenarios and not being able to stop or redirect yourself. People with GAD also experience physical symptoms of anxiety, such as fatigue, restlessness, muscle tension, and problems sleeping. Figure 6 summarizes common mental, emotional, and physical symptoms of GAD. Research suggests that older adults tend to report more physical symptoms of GAD, so pay particular attention to that aspect of GAD (Balsamo et al. 2018). These difficulties need to be present for at least six months and interfering with one's life in some way in order to receive a diagnosis of GAD. GAD tends to be one of the most common anxiety disorders experienced by older adults (Wolitsky-Taylor et al. 2010).

MENTAL	EMOTIONAL	PHYSICAL
Worry that a variety of bad things that may happen	Feeling anxious	Fatigue
	Irritability	Restlessness
Difficulty stopping worrying	Quick to anger	Muscle tension
Lack of concentration		Problems sleeping

Figure 6. These are common mental, emotional, and physical symptoms of GAD.

SOCIAL ANXIETY DISORDER: CASE EXAMPLE

Fred is a 62-year-old semiretired accountant who described himself as being a people pleaser for as long as he could remember. Fred said that he often worries about saying the wrong thing at work and offending others. He feels most anxious when he is the center of attention or when he is socializing with new people. He also tends to have difficulty saying no to people, which often results in him taking on new tasks at work when he is trying to cut back and prepare for full retirement. When he is particularly anxious, Fred tends to feel flushed and warm. As a result of his anxiety, Fred tries to avoid social gatherings and will attend them only if familiar people will be there. He also limits how much he contributes to conversations and scrutinizes what he said after interactions. Fred is concerned about how much his anxiety is impacting his social life and making things more difficult than they need to be.

Fred's experience of social anxiety disorder (SAD) is marked by having considerable anxiety in several types of social situations (for example, being the center of attention, talking to new people, or being assertive) and worrying about being judged negatively by others. People with SAD often worry about being seen as dumb, uninteresting, inarticulate, awkward, anxious, unattractive, or some variant of these things. Fred's anxiety is excessive given that there seems to be no clear reason to fear being around or judged others. We might expect that people would feel anxious over interacting with others if they were experiencing abuse or bullying, for example, and would not label this as SAD.

Fred's avoidance of social situations or only participating in them under certain circumstances (for example, with familiar people) is also very typical of social anxiety. It can seem safer to avoid them or follow particular rules for these situations (for example, only go if someone familiar will be there). At other times, people with SAD may not necessarily avoid social situations but find it very distressing and taxing to be in them. Figure 7 summarizes common mental, emotional, and physical symptoms of SAD. These difficulties need to be present for at least six months and need to be causing significant distress to an individual or impairing their lives in some way to receive a diagnosis of SAD. Interestingly, SAD is one of the least common of the anxiety disorders among older adults and tends to be more common in younger age groups (Wolitsky-Taylor et al. 2010).

MENTAL	EMOTIONAL	PHYSICAL
Worrying excessively about being judged negatively by other people in social situations	Feeling nervous before and during social situations	Feeling tense, sweaty, on edge, or flushed
		Feeling exhausted after social situations

Figure 7. These are common mental, emotional, and physical symptoms of SAD.

ILLNESS ANXIETY DISORDER: CASE EXAMPLE

Alice is an 80-year-old retired journalist who is a self-described hypochondriac. She can spend months feeling anxious about having cancer or some other serious medical issue in response to having a headache or feeling fatigued. When she feels anxious, she tends to make frequent visits to her family doctor or call her son, a physician, repeatedly. At other times, she wants to avoid any reminders of cancer, such as watching any TV shows with story lines about cancer. Alice recognizes that her worries as excessive as her family doctor has told her that she's remarkably healthy for her age aside from mild arthritis. Nonetheless, she can't seem let go of her worries that something might be very wrong with her physically. She finds it difficult to sleep when she worries about her health so much, and this often exacerbates her anxiety.

Alice's anxiety and worry is centered on having a severe medical health condition such as cancer. This is referred to as illness anxiety disorder (IAD), which was formerly called hypochondriasis. You may be thinking, *But older adults do experience more physical health problems than other age groups, isn't it normal to feel anxious about your health?* The key distinction between normal anxiety about your health and IAD is worrying *excessively*. You can identify an excessive illness worry when symptoms of the condition you're worrying about are either mild or nonexistent. If someone does have mild physical symptoms, they typically have a simpler explanation, such as fatigue or anxiety. Like many individuals with IAD, Alice often worries about her health and has a difficult time stopping. IAD can involve excessive help-seeking behaviors such as frequent visits to the doctor, endlessly researching symptoms online, or repeatedly checking one's body. Alternatively, IAD can also involve avoiding certain situations such as going to the doctor or avoiding reminders of the health condition the person is worrying about (for example, reading newspaper articles or talking about cancer). Figure 8 summarizes common mental, emotional, and physical symptoms of IAD. These difficulties need to be present for at least six months and need to be causing significant distress to an individual or impairing their lives in some way to be diagnosed with IAD.

MENTAL	EMOTIONAL	PHYSICAL
Worrying often about having or developing a serious illness	Feeling anxious when reminded of possible health problems	Fatigue
		Restlessness
Seeking information about your health excessively		Avoiding seeking help or seeking help too much

Figure 8. These are common mental, emotional, and physical symptoms of IAD.

PANIC DISORDER: CASE EXAMPLE

Jim is a 74-year-old, retired firefighter who recently made a trip to the hospital due to fears that he was having a heart attack. He told the doctor that on several occasions over the past two months he suddenly felt his heart race "out of nowhere" and felt short of breath, dizzy, and nauseous. The feelings lasted for about five minutes but frightened Jim tremendously as he thought he may pass out or even die. He first experienced the physical sensations when he was in a movie theater, and since then, he has avoided being in theaters or other spaces where it would be difficult to escape. He is even reluctant to be outside his home without his partner, in the event that he has another episode. He has sworn off physical exercise due to fears that he might provoke these feelings further. After medical investigation, Jim was informed by his doctor that he was very physically healthy and did not show any signs of heart problems.

Jim has symptoms of panic disorder, which involves having frequent panic attacks. These are intense but short-lived physical sensations of anxiety such as rapid heart rate, difficulties breathing, dizziness, feeling as if one is choking, nausea, blurred vision, or feeling as if you are removed from your body. These episodes can also include a fear of dying, fainting, going "crazy," or losing control. They typically come on out of the blue as opposed to being caused by a stressful event (for example, a car accident or public speaking). Panic attack symptoms can vary from person to person, but they usually consist of four of more of the symptoms mentioned above. Panic attacks can feel very scary, so understandably, people usually worry about when the next attack will occur. Jim started avoiding things, such as exercise, because of his panic attacks.

This is typical of panic disorder and often due to the belief these activities will cause more panic attacks. Jim avoids going places where he would not be able to escape or would not have help available if he were to experience a panic attack. This is referred to as *agoraphobia,* which may or may not accompany panic disorder. Please note that if you fear driving or falling, you would not necessarily have panic disorder unless you also experience panic attacks and fear having one in either of these circumstances. Finally, due to many of the symptoms of panic attacks resembling physical health issues (for example, tachycardia, hypoglycemia, asthma, or menopause) it is important for older adults to get medical attention to help rule out medical causes of the symptoms. Figure 9 summarizes common mental, emotional, and physical symptoms of panic disorder.

MENTAL	EMOTIONAL	PHYSICAL
Worrying about when the next panic attack will occur	Feeling scared of panic sensations	Frequent, abrupt, and unexpected feelings of racing heart, sweating, changes in breathing, chest pain, nausea, dizziness, hot/cold flashes, fear of dying/going crazy, or feelings of unreality
Being preoccupied with changes in physical sensations	Feeling out of control	

Figure 9. These are common mental, emotional, and physical symptoms of panic disorder.

From the overview of the anxiety disorders here, you may have seen some aspects of yourself in the case examples of Tina, Fred, Alice, or Jim. Although it's tempting to try to diagnose yourself with one of these disorders, it is important to speak to a qualified medical doctor, psychologist, or psychiatrist to confirm a diagnosis. It's worth noting that for all of the anxiety disorder diagnoses mentioned here, CBT is considered the gold standard of psychological treatment. So, you're in the right spot if you experience any of the difficulties we've discussed so far.

Alternatively, maybe you didn't really identify with the case examples or experience the symptoms highlighted in each section. That's perfectly ok. You might experience anxiety that is situational, that is, it is caused by a specific issue or stressor. This is normal and to be expected as people experience life changes or stressors in advancing age. CBT can still be very helpful for dealing with difficult life situations, and there are a whole host of life changes and stressors experienced in late life that can produce anxiety, such as:

- Relationships with children, grandchildren, or spouse
- Being widowed
- Caregiving responsibilities
- Chronic or acute physical health problems
- Reduced mobility or functional abilities (such as vision or hearing loss)
- Financial strain
- Relocation
- Social isolation
- Preparing for, or adjusting to, retirement
- Preparing for, or adjusting to, long-term residential care
- End-of-life concerns

That's a lot to manage. If you're in one or more of these situations, you may also notice any of the following: increased time spent worrying about the situation, difficulties concentrating or making decisions, difficulties sleeping, feeling more irritable than usual, or muscle tension or other physical symptoms of anxiety (for example, upset stomach, increased heart rate, or feeling on edge.) If this sounds like you, you're still in the right place. Remember that even if you don't have an anxiety disorder, CBT can still be helpful to you in coping with life's difficulties. Let's carry on to learn more about how.

TAKE-HOME POINTS

• *Fear and anxiety are, for the most part, useful emotions that help us deal with current and future possible dangers or threats.*

• *Anxiety becomes a problem when we feel it most of the time, worry about unlikely events, and when it causes us to engage in behaviors that are not in our best interest (such as avoidance).*

• *There are different types of anxiety disorders based on the types of worries you experience. These include:*

* *GAD: General worry about bad things happening to yourself or others*

* *SAD: Worry about being judged in social situations*

* *IAD: Worry about your physical health despite having few or no symptoms*

* *Panic disorder: Experiencing panic attacks and worrying about having more of them*

• *Anxiety can also be a normal reaction to stressful circumstances people experience as they age. If anxiety is situational, CBT can still be helpful.*

PUTTING CBT INTO PRACTICE

Complete the questionnaire below to help you identify any anxiety symptoms. The more items you rate as a 4 or 5 in each section, the more likely this is an area of concern for you.

If you notice that your score is higher than you would like it to be, rest assured, subsequent chapters will help you learn specific strategies to deal with your anxiety.

	Strongly Disagree	Disagree	Neither Agree nor Disagree	Agree	Strongly Agree
General Anxiety Disorder					
I worry about most things.	1	2	3	4	5
I worry more than most people do.	1	2	3	4	5
I have a hard time stopping worrying once I start.	1	2	3	4	5
Once I start worrying, I can't stop.	1	2	3	4	5
I feel like I can't sit still or relax.	1	2	3	4	5
I feel tired or sluggish.	1	2	3	4	5
I can't seem to focus.	1	2	3	4	5
My body feels tense.	1	2	3	4	5
Anxiety is impacting my life in a negative way.	1	2	3	4	5
Social Anxiety Disorder					
I worry about how other people think about me.	1	2	3	4	5
I feel anxious around other people despite no obvious reason to worry (for example, bullying or abuse).	1	2	3	4	5
I tend to assume other people are thinking negatively of me.	1	2	3	4	5

	Strongly Disagree	Disagree	Neither Agree nor Disagree	Agree	Strongly Agree
I feel anxious in different types of social situations (for example, parties, meeting new people, public speaking, or talking on the phone).	1	2	3	4	5
If I can get out of a social situation, I will.	1	2	3	4	5
When I have to be in social situations, I feel very uncomfortable.	1	2	3	4	5
My social anxiety is impacting my life negatively.	1	2	3	4	5

Illness Anxiety Disorder

	Strongly Disagree	Disagree	Neither Agree nor Disagree	Agree	Strongly Agree
I often worry about what could go wrong with my physical health.	1	2	3	4	5
I worry about worst-case health scenarios (for example, cancer or dementia) even if I don't experience them.	1	2	3	4	5
I try to avoid things that make me think about my health (for example, going to the doctor or reading about disease/illness).	1	2	3	4	5
I need reassurance from others about my health worries.	1	2	3	4	5
I check my body or resources online when I feel worried about my health.	1	2	3	4	5
My health anxiety is impacting my life negatively.	1	2	3	4	5

Panic Disorder

	Strongly Disagree	Disagree	Neither Agree nor Disagree	Agree	Strongly Agree
I have had multiple panic attacks.	1	2	3	4	5
My panic attacks come out of nowhere.	1	2	3	4	5

	Strongly Disagree	Disagree	Neither Agree nor Disagree	Agree	Strongly Agree
I am scared by my panic attacks.	1	2	3	4	5
My panic attacks are short-lived (at most ten minutes).	1	2	3	4	5
I am worried about when the next panic attack will occur.	1	2	3	4	5
I'm doing things differently because of my panic attacks (for example, avoiding situations or substances).	1	2	3	4	5
My panic attacks are limiting my life.	1	2	3	4	5

*Note: Panic attacks consist of at least *four* or more of the following symptoms: palpitations, pounding heart, or accelerated heart rate; sweating; trembling or shaking; shortness of breath; feeling of choking; chest pain or discomfort; nausea or abdominal distress; feeling dizzy, unsteady, lightheaded, or faint; feelings of unreality; feeling of being detached from oneself; fear of losing control or "going crazy;" fear of dying; numbness or tingling sensations; or chills or hot flushes.

WHAT'S NEXT?

- *The next chapter will focus specifically on depression. We will define what depression is, how it differs from sadness and grief, and how depression is diagnosed in older adults.*
- *You will also have a chance to self-identify any symptoms of depression that you experience.*

CHAPTER 3

Getting to Know Depression

- *Sadness is a universal human emotion that alerts us to a loss that has occurred and provides us with information about the people and things that are most important to us.*
- *Depression is a condition more severe and lengthy than sadness that negatively impacts one's life.*
- *Depression can be a challenge to diagnose in late life due to shared symptoms with physical health problems. It can also occur at the same time as older adults experience physical illness and disability.*

Now that you have a better understanding of anxiety, it's time to learn more about depression. The term depression gets used often and without a clear distinction of what it is and how it differs from regular old sadness. In this chapter, we'll highlight some of the key differences between sadness and depression and why feeling sad is normal and may, surprisingly, be useful at times. We'll review the symptoms of depression and how they present in a case example of an older adult. We'll define grief and explain how it differs from sadness and clinical depression. Then, we'll discuss how depression shouldn't be considered a normal part of aging and how research points to the exact opposite conclusion—getting older doesn't inevitably mean you get depressed. And even when depression is a challenge for older adults, it can be successfully treated. Older adults can and do benefit from CBT for depression, which means it doesn't have to cast a shadow on your later years. You can still live a healthy, vibrant, and engaged life.

Diagnosing depression in late life can be more complicated because there are some physical health conditions that may resemble depression. Older adults tend to experience more physical health problems, on average, relative to younger age groups. Later in the chapter, we'll highlight how the symptoms of depression can overlap with different medical conditions and also how depression can occur with various physical health issues.

WHY DO WE FEEL SAD?

Conventional wisdom has often encouraged us to cheer up when we feel sad. Sadness is not usually a feeling we welcome or see as being meaningful—and rightly so, given that it can make us feel heavy, slow, drained, or deflated and can even heighten our experience of physical pain. Why on earth would we have evolved to experience an emotion like sadness when, on the surface, it doesn't seem to serve any positive purpose? When we discussed the nature of anxiety, we highlighted how it plays a role in our survival, alerting us to possible dangers or threats. Can the same be said for sadness? Does it offer us any important information to help us live our lives more fully?

To help answer this question, think of the most recent time you felt sad. Where were you? What were you doing? What was going on? Perhaps it was just after seeing your grandkids pull out of your driveway after a great weekend visit. Perhaps you learned that a friend passed away. Alternatively, maybe you got the news that your hearing is getting worse and you'll be needing hearing aids soon. Do these situations have anything in common?

Although it may not be immediately obvious, one thing they share is experiencing a *loss*. The weekend is over, and the grandkids have left. A friend is no longer alive and a part of your life. Your hearing isn't what it used to be, and you need more help. Sadness can signal that we have lost something (such as a person, our independence, or an aspect of our identity) or that something good is now over (such as a career, a vacation, or a visit with grandkids). Sadness is important because it provides us with information about who and what is most important to us and what we value. Feeling sad upon retiring, for example, can signal how important having a career and workplace was to our sense of self and well-being. You might not have thought of sadness this way—a lot of us don't often hear this part of it acknowledged—but if we were to never feel sad, we would be less aware of what our values, priorities, and passions are.

What do you typically do when you feel sad? From the examples above, you might reach out to a close friend to tell them about the good visit you had with the grandkids or get busy planning the next visit. In the case of losing a friend, you may decide to go to the funeral and support the family members of the deceased. In response to needing hearing aids, you may opt to get the Mercedes Benz of hearing aids, so that you can hear as best as you can.

Are there any similarities in these responses? One common reaction to sadness is seeking comfort or connection with other people to help alleviate how we're feeling, for example, by talking to a friend or being in community with other people who may be mourning. Sadness has a unique way of bringing people closer together. Second, sadness usually prompts us to try to recover our losses as best as we can. Getting the best hearing aids possible is one example of this. Taken together, sadness may be more valuable to experience than conventional wisdom holds. It tells us who and what is most important and nudges us to connect with others and attempt to recoup our losses. In the face of life's many ups and downs and inevitable losses, remember that sadness's agenda is one of healing and resilience.

Take a moment to reflect on examples when feeling sad prompted you to take action that was helpful to you and write one down. For example, missing your colleagues from your working days led you to set up a lunch date with them, or not being able to go on a hike because of a bad knee prompted you to schedule a game night with your hiking friends.

WHAT IS DEPRESSION?

While sadness can be an adaptive emotion, depression is not. Depression is when sadness becomes malignant. Kay Redfield Jamison (1997) described depression in her memoir *An Unquiet Mind: A Memoir of Moods and Madness* as a "bleak, despairing, desperate, and deadened state ... All bearings are lost; all things are dark and drained of feeling." It's a fitting description of a mental disorder that is the leading cause of disability worldwide (World Health Organization 2021). Let's consider more specifically how depression can differ from sadness.

Your mood is consistently low. Depression involves experiencing low mood most of the day, nearly every day, for a period of two weeks or more. This is different from sadness, which ebbs and flows depending on life circumstances. Sadness typically doesn't last most of the day, nearly every day, or for weeks or months on end.

Your mood alters your behavior negatively. Depression can rob people of their motivation and energy do things that normally help them feel good. As a result, they may start to withdraw from socializing, put off doing tasks or chores, or have a difficult time taking care of themselves. Sadness, in contrast, usually prompts us to seek comfort in others or in things that make us feel good. It doesn't usually result in us withdrawing from our lives or interfere with doing the things we need to do.

Your mood affects your concentration or decision-making. Have you ever had too many programs running on your computer only to realize that everything is slowing down? That's a bit like depression. It can slow your attention and concentration and make it hard to make relatively simple decisions. As a result, it may become more difficult or time-consuming to do things that require more cognitive effort, such as reading, organizing your time, or making a decision. Sadness, on the other hand, typically doesn't have a significant impact on our ability to concentrate or make decisions.

Your mood is interfering with important aspects of your life. If it wasn't already evident from the above points, depression can wreak havoc on your life. Changes in behavior while depressed can compound and result in fractured relationships, declines in physical health, financial strain or hardship, and overall decreased quality of life. This is not usually the case for sadness as the feeling tends to be short-lived and doesn't result in more significant problems in people's lives.

In sum, depression differs from sadness in the length and severity of symptoms, and to what extent they impact someone's life. It is a serious mental health problem that can decrease quality of life and for individuals who are suicidal be life-threatening. A formal diagnosis of depression in the DSM is called a major depressive episode (MDE) and can be diagnosed only by a qualified mental health professional. Let's turn to how clinical depression may present in an older adult and discuss how it is diagnosed.

DID YOU KNOW...

The earliest accounts of depression were in the second millennium B.C.E. in Mesopotamia. At the time, it was believed to be caused by demonic possession and treated by priests or spiritual healers.

DEPRESSION: CASE EXAMPLE

Victor is a 64-year-old, divorced, retired lawyer who relocated from his home in a large city to the suburbs to be closer to his daughter, son-in-law, and two grandchildren. Victor has had several periods of time in his life when his mood was very low for months at a time. It has typically happened when he was working on high-pressure cases at work. He would feel very down and struggle to get through each week.

When he retired, he thought he'd be done with the stress, and his mood would improve. He also thought that moving to be closer to his daughter and grandkids would help. But since the move four months ago, he noticed that he has been feeling worse and worse. He wakes up most days feeling down and sad for no apparent reason and tends to feel this way for most of the day.

Victor finds it very difficult to get up in the morning and tends to stay in bed unless he has an appointment or obligation to his family. On several occasions, he's been late to his grandkids' soccer games, which upset his daughter and made Victor feel very guilty. He feels like he just can't seem to summon the motivation or energy to get up and do much of anything. He's noticed that his sleep has been much different than usual. Victor can't seem to fall asleep until 2a.m. and then sleeps in until 9a.m. or 10a.m. He tends to nap during the day because he feels overtired and just can't seem to stay awake.

Although Victor usually has a good appetite, in the past four months he hasn't felt much like eating and has lost weight. He doesn't feel very motivated to make meals, so he tends to snack during the day and eats dinner when he's at his daughter's place.

While Victor was a voracious reader during his career, he's had a difficult time concentrating enough to even read a magazine, let alone a book. He used to enjoy playing the guitar, but now any time he picks it up, it just doesn't feel as good as it did before, and he will play for only a few minutes at a time. This upsets him as he feels like he's being lazy and not doing enough during the day. Victor has felt increasingly down on himself for how little he is doing, especially after his daughter made a comment about how he is "wasting his retirement." He tends to feel like a failure and ruminate about his past mistakes and shortcomings. At times, Victor wishes he could just go to sleep and never wake up.

Victor's experiences are all too common with clinical depression. Feeling persistently down, nearly every day for at least two weeks or more is central to the experience of this disorder.

Along with feeling down most of the time, people with clinical depression find it difficult to enjoy things that they normally would. For example, Victor doesn't experience the same pleasure that he used to in playing the guitar.

Clinical depression can involve a lack of motivation or drive to do things, which Victor clearly experienced and made it difficult for him to get more accomplished during the day. Changes in sleep and appetite are common in clinical depression. People can be eating more or less than usual and sleeping more or less than usual. Victor was going to bed and sleeping later than usual and had less of an appetite. It is more common for older adults with depression to report experiencing more of the physical symptoms of this disorder, such as lack of energy or changes in sleep or appetite, than younger adults typically do (Rodda, Walker, & Carter 2011).

One unfortunate biproduct of this is that clinical depression in older adults can get sometimes get misdiagnosed as a medical issue (Kessler et al. 2010).

Cognitive changes can occur in clinical depression as well. For example, people with clinical depression can have difficulties concentrating or making decisions. Victor's struggles to concentrate long enough to read a book are an example of this. Feelings of worthlessness or excessive guilt can be part of the experience of clinical depression. People can feel very critical of themselves and have a hard time recognizing their strengths or assets. Victor indicated that he felt lazy, saw himself as not good enough, and tended to focus on his past mistakes.

Victor's desire to go to sleep and never wake up would be considered a suicidal thought, which is unfortunately common in this disorder. Clinical depression is a strong risk factor for dying by suicide. At particular risk are older adult men. Their deaths by suicide are four times as high as the national rate (Conwell & Thompson 2008). Finally, clinical depression is diagnosed when there is a clear impact of the disorder on someone's life. In Victor's case, his symptoms of depression are resulting in conflict with his daughter, difficulties taking care of himself physically, and detracting from his quality of life.

DID YOU KNOW...

Research suggests that some protective factors for suicide in late life are a sense of belonging, satisfaction with relationships, feeling useful, and religious activity (Holm & Severinsson 2015).

Figure 10 lists some common mental, emotional, and physical symptoms of depression. It is important to remember that clinical depression is not a life sentence. What Victor is experiencing can be treated. It is possible to limit the extent to which depression impacts your later years.

MENTAL	EMOTIONAL	PHYSICAL
Difficulties concentrating, focusing, or remembering things	Feeling down most of the time for at least two weeks	Moving more slowly than usual
Thinking negatively of yourself and the future	Experiencing very little pleasure or enjoyment	Sleeping more or less than usual
Having thoughts of suicide	Feeling agitated	Eating more or less than usual

Figure 10. These are common mental, emotional, and physical symptoms of depression.

HOW DOES DEPRESSION DIFFER FROM GRIEF?

So where does grief fit into the picture? Grief refers to the emotional pain that comes after the loss of someone or a something important (for example, a pet, a job, or a relationship). Similar to sadness, grief is a universal and normal part of the human experience. Case in point, mourning and associated rituals are observed in nearly every culture around the world.

Grief may feel different depending on the person, but some things people can experience are emotions such as sadness, regret, anger, or guilt; being tearful; difficulties eating or sleeping; physical aches and pains; feeling empty or numb; being disconnected from others; and lacking direction or purpose. If you've ever lost someone or something important to you, you can probably identify with some of these symptoms or recognize others that you experienced. It is important to know that there is no specific process that people *should* work through to grieve and no one way to grieve properly. Nor is there a timeline for when people should be done grieving. People work through their grief in their own way and on their own schedule.

There is some overlap between sadness and the experience of grief. Sadness is an emotion that can be experienced as part of the grieving process. Grief, however, tends to encompass a broader range of feelings and experiences than sadness, such as lacking purpose, feeling disconnected from others, physical ailments, and emotions such as anger, regret, or guilt. Grief tends to be longer lasting than sadness, which, as we discussed earlier, is typically short-lived.

DID YOU KNOW...

The parts of the brain that activate when we feel emotional pain, such as grief, are the same parts of the brain that activate when we feel physical pain.

How about the difference between grief and clinical depression? This is a matter of degree and severity. As previously covered, the symptoms of clinical depression include consistently low mood, changes to sleep and appetite, disrupted attention or concentration, difficulties making decisions, feelings of guilt or worthlessness, and suicidal thoughts or behaviors. These symptoms need to occur most of the time and be severe enough to interfere with someone's life in a significant way. It is possible that someone who is grieving could also be experiencing an episode of clinical depression. It is recommended that you seek help from a qualified mental health professional in order to make that determination.

To help summarize the difference between sadness, grief, and clinical depression, it can be helpful to think of a continuum with sadness at one end, clinical depression on the other, and grief somewhere in the middle. For those of you who feel that you may be struggling with grief, perhaps because your circumstances in life are changing or you've experienced the loss of an important person or relationship—you've picked up the right book. Many of the strategies in CBT can be very useful for coping with the continuum of grief, sadness, and clinical depression. That being said, when issues with grief or clinical depression are particularly severe, self-help resources such as this book will not likely be enough to help. Treatment from a mental health professional may be warranted when someone's grief or clinical depression is to an extent that interferes with daily life or is causing frequent thoughts of suicide. If this sounds like you, please speak to a physician and consider getting help from a mental health professional.

ISN'T AGING DEPRESSING?

You might be wondering: isn't depression common or even expected as people get older? It's a common stereotype that growing older involves experiencing losses, being sad, and generally feeling that one's life is in a state of decline. There is some truth to this stereotype, in that physical health, mobility, and independence all change as people grow older. Loss of loved ones occurs, as do changes in roles and relationships that can be difficult to cope with. All this makes it tempting to assume that older adults may experience sadness more often or have higher rates of depression than other age groups.

However, there has been some interesting research examining this very assumption. Surprisingly, the rates of depression tend to decrease as people grow older (Kessler et al. 2010). One related finding that may partially explain this trend is that older adults tend to pay attention to and remember positive information more than negative information. This is called the *positivity effect* (Carstensen & Mikels 2005). Younger adults tend to do the opposite. They pay attention to and remember negative information more than positives (Carstensen & DeLiema 2018). The bias toward positives that happens in late life can help older adults feel better emotionally. Plus, as it turns out, there is research suggesting that adults tend to experience fewer negative emotions as they grow older (Charles, Reynolds, & Gatz 2001). So, the stereo-type of older adults being sad and depressed isn't the full story. While there are elements of growing older that can be sad and challenging, there are cognitive and emotional changes in late life that may help older adults be more resilient.

DID YOU KNOW...

One reason that older adults may experience fewer negative emotions has to do with how our time perspective changes as we get older. As we perceive time is running out, we tend to focus on the present more and do what feels good in the here and now (Carstensen & Mikels 2005).

Not only does growing older bring unique emotional changes, but it also may be a time when mental health improves for some. The later years of life can prompt people to reflect on the life experiences they've had and the wisdom they've acquired. It may also be a time of freedom from the responsibilities that concern younger or middle-aged adults (such as child-rearing, building a career, or saving for retirement).

So, although experiencing loss is common with advancing age, most people will adapt and cope reasonably well with the sadness or grief that they experience. Conversely, for individuals who struggle more with their mood in late life and are diagnosed with depression, this is by no means a life sentence. Effective treatments such as CBT exist and are available. It is very much possible to improve your mental health and get back to living life how you want to.

DEPRESSION AND PHYSICAL HEALTH PROBLEMS IN LATE LIFE

Part of the challenge in diagnosing depression is that it can resemble other medical conditions. There are a number of physical health problems that older adults may experience that share some of the symptoms of clinical depression. For example, symptoms of hypothyroidism (an underactive thyroid) or vitamin B12 deficiency can include low energy, lack of motivation, and fatigue, symptoms that all overlap with clinical depression. Several types of dementia can also present similarly to depression in the early stages of the disease. Alzheimer's disease can cause apathy, social withdrawal, lack of interest in activities, and difficulties concentrating. Because of the overlap between symptoms of depression and other medical issues, it is important for older adults to get a thorough physical examination to rule out any possible physical causes of their symptoms.

To make matters even messier, clinical depression can occur alongside physical health problems that many older adults experience. It is common for adults with diabetes, heart disease, stroke, renal disease, and Parkinson's disease (among many other conditions) to feel depressed. Each of these conditions can be accompanied by major life changes and losses that can result in feeling not in control of your body or life, more dependent on others, not like yourself, and hopeless about the future. When people experience clinical depression and a major physical health issue, it can be that much harder for them to do the things they need to do to take care of their physical health, such as attend medical appointments, engage in physical exercise, maintain a balanced diet, and get sufficient sleep. This is all the more reason to pursue treatment for clinical depression if you're dealing with this condition alongside a physical health issue.

If all of this is sounding a little, well, depressing, know that by reading this book you are taking matters into your own hands and changing the course of your mental health. You can use the strategies in this book to help you feel more like your wonderful self again. It is possible to recover from depression with the right help and support. So, if you're struggling, you are in the right place.

TAKE-HOME POINTS

• *Sadness is a normal emotion that occurs when we have experienced a loss or when something enjoyable is over. When it prompts us to recoup our losses and/or seek comfort in others, it can be adaptive.*

• *Depression is maladaptive because it is more severe and prolonged than sadness and disrupts several aspects of life. It should not be considered a normal part of aging as most older adults do not experience clinical depression.*

• *Grief is what people experience when they mourn the loss of someone or something they love. It includes a broader range of emotions and experiences aside from just sadness.*

• *Clinical depression can share symptoms with a variety of medical health issues, such as dementia, and it can co-occur with a number of physical health problems. It is important to get a thorough medical examination to get an accurate diagnosis and timely treatment.*

• *Depression doesn't have to be an inevitable part of growing older. Effective treatments and supports exist. You are changing the course of your mental health by learning about and practicing CBT strategies.*

PUTTING CBT INTO PRACTICE

Complete the questionnaire below to help you identify any depression symptoms. The more items you rate as a 4 or 5, the more likely this is an area of concern for you. If you notice that your score is higher than you would like it to be, rest assured subsequent chapters in the book will help you learn specific strategies to deal with your depression. You are taking an important step in getting better.

	Strongly Disagree	Disagree	Neither Agree nor Disagree	Agree	Strongly Agree
Answer these questions in relation to the past two weeks.					
I'm feeling down or blue.	1	2	3	4	5
I don't feel like doing most things.	1	2	3	4	5
Things don't provide me pleasure like they used to.	1	2	3	4	5
I'm eating more than I used to.	1	2	3	4	5
I'm eating less than I used to.	1	2	3	4	5
I'm sleeping more than I used to.	1	2	3	4	5
I'm sleeping less than I used to.	1	2	3	4	5
I am moving slowly or like I'm going through mud.	1	2	3	4	5
I am feeling wound up.	1	2	3	4	5
I am feeling tired or worn out.	1	2	3	4	5
I am not worth much at all.	1	2	3	4	5
I feel badly for things that I have done.	1	2	3	4	5
I can't focus on what I'm doing.	1	2	3	4	5
I have a hard time making decisions for myself.	1	2	3	4	5

	Strongly Disagree	Disagree	Neither Agree nor Disagree	Agree	Strongly Agree
I think I would be better off dead.	1	2	3	4	5
I have thought about how I would take my own life.*	1	2	3	4	5

*If you have chosen a 4 or 5 for this item, please contact your family physician to discuss. immediate treatment options.

WHAT'S NEXT?

- *The next chapter will discuss the role of setting goals in cognitive behavioral therapy and how this will help manage your depression and anxiety.*
- *You will learn how to set goals that are flexible, achievable, specific, and timely.*
- *We will discuss how people can have mixed feelings about changing and how to explore any ambivalence you feel.*

PART II

Using CBT to Transform Anxiety and Depression in Later Life

CHAPTER 4

Setting Goals

- *Setting goals are an integral part of CBT. Goals identify what changes are desired and how they will be achieved.*
- *Effective goals are flexible, achievable, specific, and timely.*
- *Contrary to popular belief, people can still readily change as they grow older. Goal-setting is still important and effective.*
- *It is normal to have mixed feelings about changing. These mixed feelings can be explored using the decisional balance exercise.*

Imagine for a moment that you've decided to take a road trip. Your bags are packed, you've got plenty of snacks for the car, and your favorite music is cued up. You put your sunglasses on and shift the car into drive only to realize you have a small problem—you have no idea where you're going. No destination means no route, and no route means you have no clue how long this trip is going to take. You may want to keep the car in the driveway for the moment.

Embarking on a program of behavior change without setting a goal for where you want to be at the end of it is much like going on a road trip without a destination or route. Cognitive behavioral therapy considers goal-setting to be important for several reasons. First, goals define an outcome you're working toward. Someone struggling with anxiety may set goals to reduce time spent worrying or to overcome avoidance behaviors, for example, by driving on the highway again. They've defined success as reducing worry and stopping avoidance of certain situations. With depression, the goal may be to engage in more active tasks that bring a sense of accomplishment or pleasure. Having preset goals such as these provides direction for desired outcomes. This is akin to selecting your road-trip destination.

Second, goals define what exactly you're planning to change. For someone wanting to improve their physical fitness, they may set a goal to engage in thirty minutes of physical exercise three times a week. This goal clearly indicates what behaviors they're going to engage in and when. There's a route to the destination. Setting and reaching goals are also considered important in CBT because they impact how you feel. Reaching a goal can boost your mood, reduce your anxiety, and help you feel more confident and capable as a person. There's a multitude of reasons to be thoughtful and intentional about setting goals.

Take a moment to think of an example of a goal that defines the outcome and a specific behavior change (for example, make the majority of my meals at home by grocery shopping twice each week) and write it down.

As simple as it might sound to set goals, it is surprisingly difficult for people to both set and reach them. Look no further than New Year's resolutions. The vast majority of people who make these resolutions don't keep or achieve them. That gym membership may get used in January but be long forgotten by June. Why is it so difficult for people to set and reach their goals despite having the best of intentions? One possible reason stems from *how* people set goals. Let's say you have a goal to eat less sugar. But how much less? What types of sugar will you avoid? How exactly will you eat less? Nonspecific goals are ineffective, mainly because they leave you unsure of what steps to take. You may not end up taking any steps at all.

A second reason why people have a difficult time reaching their goals is being overambitious. You may want to be fluent in Spanish in time for your trip to Barcelona, but if you've never taken a Spanish lesson and the trip is in three weeks, that is no bueno. Overambitious goals are problematic because they typically set you up to fail and feel badly about yourself.

DID YOU KNOW...

One research study showed that one week after setting a New Year's resolution, 70 percent of people met their goal. And after two years? That number went down to 19 percent (Norcross & Vangarelli 1989). All the more reason to improve *how* you set goals.

In this chapter, we'll help define your goals for your CBT journey and you'll learn how to avoid the common mistakes that people make as they engage in goal-setting. We'll also talk about common barriers to reaching goals, such as the belief that older adults are less capable of changing and feel ambivalent about change. With this knowledge, you'll have greater clarity about what you want out of CBT. This will help you benefit more from the strategies outlined in the next few chapters.

IDENTIFYING PROBLEMS

Let's start by thinking broadly about what aspects of your life are currently affected by anxiety or depression, as the impacts can be felt across many important life areas. There are several domains of life that can be impacted by mental health difficulties, including relationships, physical health, hobbies or leisure activities, and work. By looking at how anxiety or depression are negatively impacting your life, you can start to narrow down what you'd like to be different and what goals you'd like to set.

Relationships

The impact of anxiety and depression on relationships can be varied and quite challenging. In chapter 2, you read how Fred's social anxiety resulted in him avoiding certain social gatherings and limited how he participated in them. This could start to limit the quantity and quality of his social relationships and lead him to feel lonely or disconnected from others. This can be the case for many mental disorders, which can be alienating and isolating. Loneliness is also known to negatively impact mental health and many aspects of physical health as well.

DID YOU KNOW...

Loneliness increases the risk of mortality by 26 percent, equivalent to smoking fifteen cigarettes daily (Holt-Lunstad et al. 2015).

You also read about Victor in chapter 3. His depression was starting to cause conflict with his daughter and resulting in less time spent with his grandkids. It can make you feel more depressed when you observe how your mental health is impacting important others in your life. On the flip side, having engaging, satisfying, and meaningful relationships with others can be hugely beneficial for coping with depression and anxiety. Feeling known, understood, and supported by others helps us feel more satisfied with our lives.

Physical Health

Anxiety and depression can negatively impact physical health, which may be especially detrimental in late life when people may face more issues with their physical functioning and mobility. It may be more difficult to engage in behaviors that are important for physical health, such as going to medical appointments, engaging in regular physical exercise, keeping a good sleep schedule, or eating a well-balanced diet. As older adults tend to experience more physical health difficulties, being proactive about maintaining good physical health is of utmost importance.

DID YOU KNOW...

One study demonstrated that older adults who engage in one hour of a hobby each day were at lower risk for dementia relative to those who spent thirty minutes or less (Hughes et al. 2010).

You read about Jim in chapter 2 who stopped exercising out of fear of having panic attacks, despite cardiovascular exercise being known to help reduce anxiety. You also may have noticed in the same chapter that Alice was having difficulties sleeping because of all the worrying about her health. In both cases, mental health difficulties were impacting behaviors important for physical health.

Hobbies and Leisure

Anxiety and depression may also limit your engagement in hobbies or leisure pursuits or prevent you from getting the enjoyment from them that you normally would. In chapter 2, Tina felt less able to concentrate on reading and oil painting because her worries felt distracting. Victor felt that his depression made it difficult to engage with and enjoy things he previously did, such as reading and playing the guitar.

It is especially concerning when anxiety or depression limits participation in or satisfaction derived from hobbies and leisure pursuits.

Hobbies and leisure tasks are more important than you might think for our mental health. They can boost your mood, connect you with other people, promote creativity and problem-solving, and keep you cognitively stimulated—all essential benefits as you grow older.

Work

Mental health difficulties can pose a number of challenges to engaging in meaningful work. While some older adults are retired, others are semiretired or engage in nonremunerated forms of work, such as volunteerism. Irrespective of what form of work you may or may not engage in, there's no denying the impact of depression and anxiety on people's work lives. It can result in greater absenteeism, lost wages, or reduced effectiveness at work. The impact of depression on job performance has been estimated to be greater than that of conditions such as arthritis, hypertension, back problems, and diabetes (Wells et al. 1989; Kessler et al. 2001).

Fred's social anxiety made it difficult for him to say no to work-related tasks, which likely contributed to him feeling more anxious. It may have resulted in him struggling to find the time to do it all and spending more time at work. If you are struggling with depression, you may find it difficult to feel motivated to engage in meaningful work or give your full effort. Clearly, there are a multitude of ways in which depression and anxiety can throw a wrench into the work lives of older adults. It's important to identify these issues because work has the potential to be a big source of satisfaction, fulfillment, and meaning.

From the descriptions above, you may have some idea about how anxiety or depression are impacting your life. Take a few moments to write down some of the key ways you think your own problems with anxiety or low mood impact your life across the domains listed.

Relationships: _____

Physical health: _____

Hobbies and leisure: _____

Work: _____

Other: _____

TRANSLATING PROBLEMS INTO GOALS

Now that we've begun to identify the problem, let's help you transform what you wrote above into more tangible goals. There are four features of goals that set us up for success. Effective goals tend to be flexible, achievable, specific, and timely. Let's look at each in a little more detail.

Flexible

Helpful goals are framed in a way that allows for flexibility. Let's say you've set a goal to file your taxes and you aim to spend thirty minutes every day working on them. But one day, you feel unmotivated and end up avoiding your tax work altogether. The following day you may tell yourself, *I've already blown my goal to work on it every day so why bother trying?*

It's all too common for people to abandon a goal when they perceive they've failed. We often neglect the fact that it's normal and expected that you won't be able to make consistent progress toward a goal. There will be valid reasons why you won't be able to exercise, practice a musical instrument, or prepare a healthy meal, for instance.

Instead of pretending this won't happen, it's best to plan for off days and incorporate this into your goal. One way to do this is to frame a goal as percent adherence, for example, *I will make meals at home 80 percent of the time this week.* What's the upside of this? You may be more likely to persist in your efforts to reach the goal, and you may feel less badly if you don't reach a goal on a given day or week.

Professional baseball players, the very best at what they do, have to work with the same flexible goals—a great batting average is not hitting the ball every time at bat but rather getting a hit one out of every three times at bat.

Achievable

We tend to err on the side of setting goals that are unrealistic and overly ambitious. We can set ourselves up for success by setting goals that we can, in fact, reach. If you've been meaning to clean out your garage but have been avoiding it for the past four years, it's not necessarily realistic to set the goal to clean out the entire garage within a day. Perhaps it's more realistic to set the goal to organize your power tools first.

A good litmus test of whether a goal is realistic is your reaction to seeing the goal written down on a piece of paper. Do you feel intimated or overwhelmed, or do you feel reasonably confident about your ability to reach the goal? If it's the latter, you're on the right track. If it's the former, consider breaking the goal down into smaller parts until the idea of getting started on a smaller part doesn't seem so overwhelming.

Specific

When goals are framed in a way that is vague, it can be difficult to tell when you've achieved it. If your goal is to feel less depressed, how do you know when you've met this goal? Consider framing your goals in terms of specific behavioral changes. This makes it easier to assess change and determine success.

DID YOU KNOW...

Writing down your goals can have a positive impact on how you feel emotionally. One study demonstrated how the positive benefits of writing goals down can be maintained for up to five months (King 2001).

For example, your goal may be to see one friend twice a week, go for a thirty-minute walk three times a week, or spend one hour per week preparing a will. Need some help identifying specific behaviors? You may want to answer the following question: if I am feeling at my best, what behaviors would I be doing more of or less of?

Timely

Have you ever given yourself an unlimited amount of time to complete a task only to find that you never actually complete the task? Join the club. We've all likely told ourselves, *I'll get around to that sometime,* only to find that *sometime* never rolls around. It's helpful to specify a timeline for meeting a goal, which can help kickstart you into action. For example, if your goal is to prepare dinner at 6p.m. each day for the next two weeks, it's clear *when* you will take steps toward your goal and over *what* time period.

Let's look at examples of effective goals set by Tina, Fred, Alice, Jim, and Victor. See if you can spot how they are flexible, achievable, specific, and timely.

	Goal 1	Goal 2	Goal 3
Tina	Reduce time spent worrying by 50 percent	Take a relaxing bath before bed twice a week	Oil paint for forty-five minutes once a week for the next month
Fred	Attend one social gathering alone this month	Say no to a work request this week	Share one thing about myself during a lunch with colleagues this Friday
Alice	Reduce number of calls to son about health worries by 50 percent	Watch a TV show about cancer once a week	Spend fifteen minutes journaling about health worries three times a week
Jim	Go to the grocery store without partner once a week	Go to a movie theater once this month	Ride stationary bike for twenty minutes three times a week
Victor	Get up most mornings between 8 a.m. and 8:30 a.m.	Eat at least two meals a day, most days	Play the guitar twice a week for thirty minutes

Now it's your turn. Write out your goals such that they are flexible, achievable, specific, and timely.

Goal 1	Goal 2	Goal 3

As a final suggestion for your goals: often it can be helpful to share your intention with others. Research suggests that people who share their goals with friends or family members are more likely to reach their goals.

If you have people in your life who you could share your goals with, who would those be? List one or more here.

CAN OLDER ADULTS CHANGE?

All this talk of goal-setting may have you wondering whether the effort is even worth it because older adults have a harder time changing, right? Not so fast. That is a common ageist belief that is worth inspecting more closely. It is commonly assumed that older adults are more stubborn, resistant to change, and stuck in their ways. Media depictions of older adults, particularly older men, play up this stereotype. Like most stereotypes, we can all probably find an example that confirms them.

However, they also paint a picture that isn't entirely accurate and at their worst, are harmful to those being stereotyped. Older adults who believe such ageist stereotypes can also suffer the consequences. They have lower life expectancy, higher blood pressure, reduced self-esteem, and reduced risk-taking motivation (Coudin & Alexopoulos 2010; Cruikshank 2003; Levy et al. 2000; Levy et al. 2002). One possible explanation for these findings is that if you believe in negative ageing stereotypes, they become a self-fulfilling prophecy. That is, if you believe older adults can't change, you won't push yourself to set new goals or take steps to reach them. Evidently, ageist stereotypes are not only inaccurate, but they also can be harmful to those who believe them. Actively questioning and challenging these beliefs can be empowering and lead to positive behavioral change.

DID YOU KNOW...

One effective way of challenging a stereotype is to build a personal relationship that challenges the belief. Surround yourself with older adults who have made positive changes in their lives.

The good news is that there is no evidence to support the idea that older adults are less capable of changing than younger adults. In fact, research studies examining the effectiveness of CBT, which focuses on cognitive and behavioral change, with older adults show that it is just as effective as it is with younger age groups (Karlin et al. 2015; Walker & Clarke 2001). So, there's good reason to be optimistic that you too can benefit from CBT and use it to make meaningful changes in your life.

COPING WITH AMBIVALENCE

As much as someone dealing with anxiety or depression may want to feel better and engage in treatment, they may also have conflicting feelings about it. *Ambivalence* is the state of experiencing seemingly contradictory beliefs or emotions at the same time. Ambivalence is a common feeling when people are embarking on a journey to improve their mental health. Despite this being a meaningful and impactful venture, people can have conflicting feelings about change. Ambivalence can be due to a variety of different reasons. Engaging in most treatments (such as following a medication regimen or exercising regularly)—and perhaps especially CBT—requires commitment, effort, and time. People may not want to devote the work needed to get better even though it could improve their life in the long term.

DID YOU KNOW...

Ambivalence doesn't necessarily mean you won't benefit from CBT. One study showed that ambivalence doesn't change how effective CBT is. *Resisting* change, however, does make it hard to benefit from CBT (Button et al. 2015).

Ambivalence may also stem from a fear of change. As much as people may want to reduce their anxiety or depression, doing so may also mean confronting aspects of their lives that may be difficult as opposed to avoiding them. For example, someone who wants to reduce a fear of going to the doctor will have to face this type of situation repeatedly to feel more comfortable over time. As much as improving one's mental health can improve relationships, it can sometimes cause conflict or negative changes in relationships. Case in point, someone who wants to get better at saying no to others may find that in doing so, not everyone responds positively to their newfound ability to be assertive. Like most things in life, change is complicated.

You might be tempted dismiss your ambivalence and stay focused on your goals, but in CBT we encourage people to do the opposite. Directly exploring any ambivalence about change can be a tremendous benefit as people start CBT. Why? By exploring any resistance to change we can anticipate possible barriers that may get in the way and help people reduce those barriers as much as possible.

One helpful exercise to examine any ambivalence you may have about changing is called a *decisional balance*. It involves identifying the advantages and disadvantages of changing as well as those of staying the same. This can help you understand why you may be hesitant to change but also why changing may be so important. Let's look at an example of a decisional balance completed by Victor.

Decisional Balance: Victor

	Advantages	Disadvantages
Changing	Better mood Less conflict with daughter Take better care of myself physically Enjoy my retirement more Have a better relationship with grandkids	It will take time and effort to learn new skills to improve my mood. I will have to take more responsibility for my mental health.
Staying the Same	Depression is what I know and am used to. I don't have to put in much effort	My physical health is suffering. More conflict with daughter Less quality time with grandkids Suicidal thoughts may increase.

Victor can revisit his decisional balance exercise during times when he may be feeling less motivated to change or discouraged as a way to remind himself why he is engaging in CBT and trying to change. This can be a helpful step to renew your commitment to the actions you're taking to improve your mental health.

The decisional balance exercise can also help people engage in problem-solving to reduce the barriers to change. For example, since Victor highlighted his concerns about the time and effort needed to change, he may decide to dedicate a specific time each week to implementing his CBT strategies. He may also opt to share what he is learning with his daughter to help boost his motivation to change.

TAKE-HOME POINTS

• It is important to set goals when engaged in CBT as they identify the changes you want to make and how you're going to get there. It's just like having a destination and route planned for a road trip.

• People commonly set goals that are unrealistic or vague. We are more likely to achieve goals that are flexible, achievable, specific, and timely.

• Older adults can indeed change and should continue to set goals for themselves.

• Ambivalence about change is normal and can be explored more through the decisional balance exercise.

PUTTING CBT INTO PRACTICE

Now let's have you complete your own decisional balance exercise, so that you too can explore any ambivalence you may have about changing and highlight the important reasons why you are embarking on your self-help journey.

To complete this decisional balance exercise, select one change you're thinking of making and identify the advantages and disadvantages of making that change versus staying the same. Doing so will help you identify any ambivalence you may have about changing and also solidify your reasons for engaging in CBT. You can revisit this exercise when you need a helpful reminder for why you are doing CBT and why changing is important.

Decisional Balance

	Advantages	Disadvantages
Changing		
Staying the Same		

WHAT'S NEXT?

- *The next chapter will introduce the idea of self-monitoring and explain why it is so important in order to make progress toward our goals.*
- *We will talk about how to know the difference between a thought, emotion, behavior, and physical sensation.*

CHAPTER 5

Self-Monitoring: Increasing Self-Awareness

- *Identifying your emotions, thoughts, behaviors, and physical sensations is a critical step in learning how to change your responses.*
- *Emotions are subjective experiences that provide us with information and motivate action.*
- *Thoughts are automatic and can be distorted in ways that add to anxiety and depression.*
- *Avoidance and overdoing behaviors are common when people feel anxious or depressed.*
- *Physical sensations can be a part of the emotions we experience, trigger them, or both.*

Think about a task that you do on a regular basis. Driving to your daughter's house. Walking the dog. Getting groceries. Taking a shower. Making a meal. Now try to describe that task in as much detail as possible. What thoughts were going through your head? What were you feeling in your body? What emotions were you experiencing? For many people, it can be surprisingly difficult to answer these questions.

More often than not, we are on autopilot, unaware of what's going on inside our minds and bodies. It's not necessarily a bad thing to be on autopilot. Think about how tiring it would be to be aware of every single thing you experience during a day (and who wants to be that aware when you're at the dentist). That said, being on autopilot is challenging when you want to make changes in your life to cope differently with anxiety and depression. After all, we need to be aware of what we're experiencing in order to make any meaningful changes in our thinking or behavior.

Remember that the main assumption in CBT is that that emotions, thoughts, behaviors, and physical sensations are all interrelated. We seek to make changes to our thoughts and behaviors in order to affect how we feel emotionally and physically. But we need to be aware of what is happening inside of ourselves in order to make changes to our thoughts or behaviors. That's where *self-monitoring* comes in. Self-monitoring is the act of paying attention to and noting—for example, by writing them down—your emotions, thoughts, behaviors, and physical sensations when you notice significant changes in these areas.

Interestingly, research demonstrates that simply paying attention and monitoring changes in the way we feel can lead to significant improvements in mood (Bakker & Rickard 2018). This chapter is intended to help you develop the tools needed to engage in self-monitoring so that you can be more aware of yourself and better situated to make changes to your thinking patterns and behaviors.

The process of self-monitoring is much like what scientists do when they run experiments. They gather information about what is occurring and when and then identify patterns. When you self-monitor, you'll be operating much like a scientist. You'll be observing and writing out your emotions, thoughts, behaviors, and physical sensations. This might sound fairly easy. But it can be a struggle to identify what you're thinking or feeling, and rightly so—remember that we're on autopilot most of the time. But with proper guidance going in, and patience with the process as you practice this skill, you'll find it pays off.

You may also find it challenging to know the difference between an emotion and a thought, and you wouldn't be the only one. In this chapter, we will describe and distinguish between emotions, thoughts, behaviors, and physical sensations. We'll also provide a framework to engage in self-monitoring of each of these components. By engaging in self-monitoring, you'll have greater self-awareness and insight and be better situated to make changes in how you think or behave. Let's explore emotions in more detail first.

EMOTIONS

What are emotions? There are many answers to this question depending on the expert you speak to, but most definitions of emotions highlight that they are *subjective* reactions to experiences that provide us with *information* and *motivate* us to take action. Emotions often involve physiological reactions, such as increased heart rate, stomach churning, or lethargy, that can vary depending on the type of emotion someone is experiencing.

Many universal emotions have been identified across cultures, including happiness, sadness, anger, fear, guilt, shame, disgust, and surprise. But ultimately, emotions are subjective in that how one person experiences a feeling could be different than how another person experiences it. Anxiety for one person might feel like they can't stop or slow down, whereas for another person, they may feel paralyzed by it. (Of course, there's no right or wrong way to experience an emotion.)

We've evolved to have emotions because they have historically provided us with valuable information about our external environment. We discussed how fear alerts us to the presence of danger and how sadness signals a loss that has occurred. But other emotions, such as anger, guilt, and shame, provide different and equally as important forms of information. Let's look at examples of the types of information that different emotions give us:

Emotion	Information
Happiness	This feels good.
Sadness	I've lost something or someone important.
Anger	This is wrong or unfair.
Fear	Danger!
Guilt	I've done something bad.
Shame	I am bad.
Disgust	This is gross or could be bad for me.
Surprise	This was unexpected.

Along with giving us information, our emotions prompt us to take action. The root of the word emotion is *motion,* after all. The actions they prompt us to take are linked to our survival in that they help keep us safe or help maintain our connection to others. Let's look at examples of the actions different emotions prompt us to take:

Emotion	Information
Happiness	Keep doing more
Sadness	Seek comfort, recoup losses
Anger	Right the wrong, seek justice
Fear	Flee from danger or fight it

Emotion	Information
Guilt	Repair or make amends
Shame	Hide, stay silent
Disgust	Back away
Surprise	Figure out what is happening

You may have noticed from all this talk about emotions so far that we're not labeling any emotion as negative or positive. Emotions are not inherently bad or good. They just serve different purposes. It's also important to understand that humans have evolved to experience each emotion for important reasons and you can't rid yourself of them—nor would that be in anyone's best interest. If you never felt guilt, for instance, you'd never apologize to a friend for forgetting their birthday. If you never felt angry, you'd never stand up to someone who was treating you poorly. If you never felt shame, you'd leave your house without pants on and have to answer some difficult questions from the police. Even unpleasant emotions serve a purpose.

HOW DO I IDENTIFY MY EMOTIONS?

Some people have a more difficult time than others identifying their emotions. There's a multitude of reasons why, but one that we'll highlight relates to life experiences. If you've grown up in an environment in which no one really recognized or talked about emotions, or that only permitted certain emotions to be expressed, it can be more difficult to identify and express certain emotions as an adult. For example, some older adult men may have grown up in a time where it was less acceptable to express emotions such as sadness or fear. This can lead to difficulties with recognizing and expressing these emotions and expressing others, such as anger, instead. The character of Archie Bunker in the TV show *All in the Family* is a prime example of this.

If you struggle with recognizing your emotions, there are a few strategies you can employ to help. First, you can look at a list of emotion words to help identify what you might be feeling. If we lack the language to talk about how we're feeling, having a list of words to describe our emotions can be very helpful. The list of emotion words below can be good to consult as you engage in the exercises in this chapter.

Another way to help identify your emotions is to focus on what is happening inside your body. Physical sensations can give us clues to what we might be experiencing emotionally. For example, feeling tense and agitated might mean you feel angry. Feeling lethargic and low energy might mean you're sad. Feeling tightness in your chest or stomach might mean you're anxious. Older adults tend to report more of their physical sensations when asked to describe how they're feeling emotionally (Balsamo et al. 2018; Palmer et al. 1997), so this might be a useful way for you to capture your experience, too.

A different technique you can use to identify your emotions involves imagining someone you know in the identical situation and considering what they might be feeling. For example, if you're struggling to identify your feelings after an argument with your adult son, imagine what someone else might be feeling in the same situation. It could be anger, irritation, annoyance, sadness, or confusion, for example.

Emotion Vocabulary List

Happiness	Sadness	Anger	Fear
Elated	Despair	Rage	Terror
Excited	Demoralized	Incensed	Horrified
Cheerful	Regretful	Angry	Afraid
Satisfied	Discouraged	Resentful	Scared
Content	Somber	Irritated	Anxious
Pleased	Down	Annoyed	Uneasy
Glad	Glum	Frustrated	Apprehensive

Guilt	Shame	Disgust	Surprise
Remorse	Disgraced	Repulsed	Amazement
Contrite	Ashamed	Detest	Awe
Regretful	Defective	Repugnant	Shock
Culpable	Humiliated	Loath	Appalled
Sorry	Abashed	Awful	Bewildered
Repentant		Distasteful	Perplexed
Wrong		Repugnant	Taken aback

Let's get some practice identifying your emotions using the strategies mentioned above. Pick a situation from the last week and write out where you were (for example, at home or in a coffee shop), what was going (for example, talking with partner or waiting in line). Then try to use each of the three strategies mentioned above to help identify what emotions you may have been experiencing at the time:

- Refer to list of emotion vocabulary words.
- Examine what you're feeling in your body.
- Think of what someone else might be feeling in the same situation.

An additional helpful step is to rate the intensity of the emotion(s) you're experiencing, which can help you notice nuance in what you feel.

In this worksheet, emotions are rated from 0 to 10, with 10 being the most intense. Here's an example from Tina.

Situation	Emotions (Rate intensity from 0 to 10.)
Lying in bed at 1 a.m., sleepless due to worry	Anxious (6) Annoyed (7) Tense (5)

Now try it with an example from your life. Rate each emotion from 0 to 10, with 10 being the most intense.

Situation	Emotions (Rate intensity from 0 to 10.)

Now let's discuss something that goes hand in hand with emotions—thoughts.

THOUGHTS

Alongside the emotions we experience, we also have the running commentary that is our thoughts. They are typically verbal statements or images that occur so quickly that at times, they seem automatic. Aaron Beck, the founder of CBT we discussed in chapter 1, coined the term *automatic thoughts* to refer to the thoughts that seemingly occur out of the blue and without our conscious control. Examples of automatic thoughts are: *What if something terrible happens to my grandchild? I'll be so bored when I retire. My son is concerned only about himself.* While these are all examples of negative automatic thoughts, it's important to note that we also experience plenty of positive and neutral automatic thoughts such as: *My new family doctor is very friendly. My arthritis has been better lately. I need to call the pharmacy to refill my prescription.*

Automatic thoughts are also very *subjective*, meaning they will vary from person to person, even when people are faced with the same situation. It makes sense—of course people will vary in their reaction to, and interpretation of, situations. Because of that, it's important to recognize that thoughts are not facts. To illustrate, consider the following example. You want to call your friend to set up a time to meet for lunch because you haven't seen them in a few weeks. Your call goes straight to voice mail, and you leave a message. A few days go by, and you haven't heard back from your friend. What would you be thinking?

You could have positive automatic thoughts such as *She's probably off having fun with her grandson* or *Maybe she's on vacation.* You could also have neutral automatic thoughts such as *She doesn't check her voice mail very often* or *She's probably had a busy week.* Or you could have negative automatic thoughts such as *She doesn't care about me* or *What if she's had a medical emergency?*

And depending on what types of automatic thoughts you have, your emotional reactions will vary accordingly. If you assumed your friend was off having fun with her grandson, you may feel happy for her. If you assumed she was having a medical emergency, you may feel anxious. If you assumed she doesn't care about you, you could feel hurt or annoyed. Case in point, the automatic thoughts we have influence our emotional reactions.

In CBT, we seek to increase awareness of your automatic thoughts and develop your ability to evaluate whether these thoughts are realistic or whether they help us respond to a situation effectively. We'll look at the process of questioning thoughts in the next chapter. For now, the first step is identifying what your automatic thoughts are. Let's try this out briefly. Look at the situation you wrote down in the previous exercise and the emotion that you identified. See if you can identify the automatic thoughts you may have had in that situation.

Here's an example from Tina. In this worksheet, emotions are rated from 0 to 10, with 10 being the most intense.

Situation	Emotions (Rate intensity from 0 to 10.)	Thoughts
Lying in bed at 1 a.m., sleepless due to worry	Anxious (6) Annoyed (7) Tense (5)	My grandson had a cough today. What if he has pneumonia? If I can't sleep well tonight, my day will be ruined. I'm such an idiot for forgetting my doctor's appointment today.

Now try it with an example from your life.

Situation	Emotions (Rate intensity from 0 to 10.)	Thoughts

COGNITIVE DISTORTIONS

Let's take a closer look at the thoughts you wrote down in this exercise. Do you notice any patterns or themes? Our minds can fall into rather predictable patterns of thinking that CBT calls *cognitive distortions* (Beck et al. 1979; Burns 1980). As the name implies, these thoughts can be misrepresentations of what is actually happening. It's like wearing a pair of glasses with pink lenses and concluding the world has turned a lovely shade of fuchsia.

If we look at Tina's first thought (*My grandson had a cough today. What if he has pneumonia?*), we can spot one cognitive distortion called *catastrophizing*. This refers to when we assume worst-case scenarios are occurring despite limited evidence to suggest that's the case. Although it's possible that Tina's grandson has pneumonia, she doesn't know that for sure and it may not be the most *likely* explanation for his cough.

Tina's second thought (*If I can't sleep well tonight, my day will be ruined.*) demonstrates another cognitive distortion called *black-and-white thinking*. This is when we think in dichotomous ways when there may be important nuance that we may be missing. Even if Tina doesn't sleep well tonight and is overtired tomorrow, she still may be able to do *some* things and derive pleasure from her day. It's not entirely realistic to say her day will be a complete write-off.

In Tina's last thought (*I'm such an idiot for forgetting my doctor's appointment.*), we see her falling into the cognitive distortion called *labeling* wherein people tend to label themselves (or others) in overly negative ways. Does forgetting a doctor's appointment make Tina an idiot? Or does it mean that she's a human being who sometimes makes mistakes? We tend to think the latter.

Catastrophizing, black-and-white thinking, and labeling are among many different types of cognitive distortions that people can be subject to. We summarize them below and encourage you to review them closely.

Distortion	Definition	Example
Catastrophizing	Assuming a worst-case scenario is occurring despite not having all the facts; can involve used loaded language such as *awful* or *terrible*	My headache might be a brain tumor.
Black-and-white thinking	Thinking in dichotomous ways and missing important shades of gray	If I can't do this right, there's no point in doing it.
Labeling	Using a negative label to describe oneself or others	I'm such a failure. He's so lazy.
Mental filtering	Selectively looking at the negative aspects of a situation and ignoring the positives or neutrals	I know my doctor said this medication was safe and effective, but I can't help thinking about all the possible side effects.

Distortion	Definition	Example
Mind-reading	Making negative assumptions about what someone is thinking or feeling despite not having all the facts	My son didn't respond to my text. He must be upset with me.
Should statements	Setting rigid standards or expectations for yourself or others using words such as *should, must,* or *ought*	I should be able to manage all the household chores by myself. I shouldn't be feeling so anxious about driving on the highway.

Look back at the thoughts you wrote down in this exercise. Do any of them look like cognitive distortions? There might be more than one that are relevant. Make note of which ones may be coming up in your thinking. We'll return to the idea of cognitive distortions in the next chapter, where we'll talk about how to challenge your thinking. For now, you're off to a great start identifying your emotions and your thoughts. Let's turn to the next component of the self-monitoring: identifying behaviors.

BEHAVIORS

Emotions and thoughts are deeply connected to the patterns of behavior that we engage in. As mentioned earlier in this chapter, emotions motivate action—and often, very sensibly, they drive you to avoid a situation that is genuinely dangerous. But sometimes the behaviors that we engage in related to anxiety and depression can be less helpful, such as avoiding social contact for extended periods of time. This will likely just make anxiety or depression worse over time, even if it seems like the better or easier option at the time.

People who struggle with anxiety or depression can find themselves routinely engaging in two types of behaviors. One is *avoidance behaviors*. Sometimes these behaviors are easily recognizable, such as avoiding driving on highways if you have a phobia of driving. At other times avoidance behaviors can be more subtle, such as trying to distract yourself so you don't feel your anxiety. The other type of behavior that can be connected to anxiety and depression is *overdoing*. This can consist of doing a range of things in excess, such as seeking reassurance, overplanning, repeatedly checking, or researching intensely.

Below we highlight more examples of what might fall into either category. Place a checkmark beside which behaviors you notice yourself engaging in when you're distressed.

Avoidance Behaviors	✓	Overdoing Behaviors	✓
Avoiding a situation		Overplanning the future	
Procrastinating on a task		Making excessive to-do lists	
Trying not to think about something		Seeking reassurance	
Saying no to social invites or activities		Spending considerable time researching a topic	
Partially committing to things		Refusing to delegate tasks	
Distracting yourself to not think or feel something		Spending excessive amounts of time working on a task	
Avoiding topics of conversation		Oversharing personal information with others	
Using alcohol or substances		Giving unsolicited advice to others	
Staying in bed or sleeping longer than usual		Checking on someone or something repeatedly	
Avoiding being in situations alone or without a support person		Excessively monitoring the focus of a worry (such as the stock market or blood pressure)	

Many of these behaviors, when considered in context of the thoughts and emotions you experience, make compete sense. They are intended help protect you from negative emotions. If you checked off any of the behaviors above, take a second to pick one and see if you can figure out what negative emotions you might have been trying to protect yourself from the last time you practiced it. Write them down.

If you are anxious and assuming you're going to hear terrible news from your doctor at your next appointment, of course you're going to want to avoid it. If you feel depressed and think you're incapable of doing anything right, of course you're not going to want to make an effort to try new things or get out of the house. In the short term, engaging in these behaviors might help you feel better. Most people are relieved to avoid unpleasant emotions.

Often, however, the behaviors that make us feel better in the short term can make us feel worse in the long term. If you are depressed and avoiding social interactions, for instance, you're missing out on opportunities to boost your mood and feel more connected to others, and this may contribute to you feeling depressed. Social interactions, especially those that provide emotional support, are also incredibly important for cognitive functioning in late life (Seeman et al. 2001). Consequently, avoidance of social relationships as an older adult is problematic from psychological, emotional, and cognitive perspectives.

If you are procrastinating, you may just be prolonging your worry and adding additional stress when you run short on time to complete something. If you spend an inordinate amount of time planning and researching, you may feel more anxious and irritated when things don't go according to plan or aren't exactly what you expected. If you use alcohol to help soothe negative feelings, you might continue to feel the same way the next day given that alcohol tends to depress people's moods. Older adults are particularly vulnerable to the negative effects of alcohol (Moos et al. 2010).

Consider again that experience of avoidance behaviors or overdoing you just wrote about. Were there longer-term consequences for reacting in this way, even if in the short term, you were able to avoid or deal with negative emotions at the time? If so, write them down.

The key point here is the behaviors we engage in have a direct impact on our emotions and thoughts. Identifying what behaviors you engage in when you experience certain emotions and thoughts is a critical step before learning how to change your behavior. Return to the example you wrote down earlier in which you identified your emotions and thoughts and add what behaviors you engaged in and try to categorize them as either avoidance or overdoing.

In this worksheet, emotions are rated on a scale of 0 to 10, with 10 being the most intense. Here are Tina's responses as an example.

Situation	Emotions (Rate intensity from 0 to 10.)	Thoughts (Include any distortions.)	Behavior (Categorize if avoidance or overdoing.)
Lying in bed at 1 a.m., sleepless due to worry	Anxious (6) Annoyed (7) Tense (5)	My grandson had a cough today. What if he has pneumonia? (catastrophizing) If I can't sleep well tonight, my day will be ruined. (all or nothing thinking) I'm such an idiot for forgetting my doctor's appointment today. (labeling)	Look up symptoms of pneumonia online (overdoing) Distract by watching TV (avoidance) Triple-check next appointment time and call office to reconfirm (overdoing)

Now try it with an example from your life. Rate emotions on a scale of 0 to 10, with 10 being the most intense.

Situation	Emotions (Rate intensity from 0 to 10.)	Thoughts (Include any distortions.)	Behavior (Categorize if avoidance or overdoing.)

Finally, let's examine how physical sensations fit into the process of self-monitoring our emotions, thoughts, and behaviors.

PHYSICAL SENSATIONS

You might be wondering why in a book about anxiety and depression we would be talking about monitoring physical sensations. Well, it turns out that you can't separate mind and body. The two are irrevocably linked. As we mentioned when we discussed emotions, there are oftentimes physiological sensations we experience as part of our emotional reactions. For example, sadness might be accompanied by lethargy or sluggishness. Anxiety can be accompanied by an upset stomach or restlessness. The physical sensations people experience are unique to each person. One person might experience an upset stomach when they feel anxious, whereas another person might notice muscle tension.

Many of the physiological sensations we experience when we have emotions are linked to the evolutionary purpose of the emotion. We discussed in chapter 2 how when people feel anxious, this activates their fight-flight-freeze response, which is a cascade of different bodily reactions such as increased heart rate, changes in breathing, light-headedness, and sweating. All of these physical sensations indicate that our body is redirecting biological resources, such as oxygen, to places in the body where it is needed in order for someone to run away from or fight the danger that is potentially in front of them. Our emotions and physiology are often working in coordination to help us deal with the situation we're in.

At other times, physical sensations may be the trigger for certain thoughts, emotions, and behaviors. People who have panic attacks and experience rapid heart rate or shortness of breath, for example, may think *I'm having a heart attack,* feel more panicked as a result, and seek medical attention. As another example, a person dealing with bladder or bowel control issues might feel anxious when they feel the need to use a bathroom in public. They may think, *What if I have an accident in public and embarrass myself?* and avoid being in public spaces for very long or always stay close to a bathroom. Or another person dealing with chronic pain might think, *I'm not able to live my life the way I want to,* feel demoralized, and start to disengage from certain activities. With various changes in physical health, mobility, and functionality that can occur in late life, it is common for our physical bodies to trigger a wide range of emotional and cognitive reactions.

Although we can't always control the physical sensations we experience, we do have a say over our reaction to them. It starts when we become aware of those sensations as they arise. So, let's add physical sensations to the process of self-monitoring you've been working with.

Here is Tina's example again. In this worksheet, emotions are rated from 0 to 10, with 10 being the most intense.

Situation	Emotions (Rate intensity from 0 to 10.)	Thoughts	Behavior	Physical Sensations
Lying in bed at 1 a.m., sleepless due to worry	Anxious (6) Annoyed (7) Tense (5)	My grandson had a cough today. What if he has pneumonia? (catastrophizing) If I can't sleep well tonight, my day will be ruined. (all or nothing) I'm such an idiot for forgetting my doctor's appointment today. (labeling)	Look up symptoms of pneumonia online Distract by watching TV Triple-check next appointment time and call office to reconfirm	Tension in jaw Restlessness Pit in stomach

Now try it with an example from your life. Rate emotions on a scale of 0 to 10, with 10 being the most intense.

Situation	Emotions (Rate intensity from 0 to 10.)	Thoughts	Behavior	Physical Sensations

There you have it. Hopefully, by now, you are more aware of why self-monitoring is so important and how to recognize your own emotions, thoughts, behaviors, and physical sensations more effectively. This is a critical stepping stone on your way to changing how you think and behave, and better managing your anxiety and depression.

TAKE-HOME POINTS

- *In order to make changes within ourselves, we need to identify our emotions, thoughts, behaviors, and physical sensations.*
- *Emotions can be identified by examining what we feel inside, using a list of emotion vocabulary words, or considering what someone else would be feeling in the same circumstance.*
- *Thoughts play a big role in influencing our emotions. Thoughts aren't facts, however. They can sometimes contain cognitive distortions, such as all-or -nothing thinking or catastrophizing.*
- *The behaviors we engage in when we feel anxious or depressed, such as avoidance or overdoing, are designed to reduce negative emotions in the short term but can do the opposite in the long term.*
- *Physical sensations go hand in hand with the emotions, thoughts, and behaviors we experience. They can be a trigger for, or a reaction to, our emotions, thoughts, and behaviors.*

PUTTING CBT INTO PRACTICE

Continue to be a scientist and gather more information on your emotions, thoughts, behavior, and physical sensations that arise in a variety of situations over the coming week and note them in the Self-Monitoring Log below. Try to complete one entry per day. The more you practice, the more you become more aware of what's going on. This will situate you to implement the strategies in upcoming chapters and make changes in how you think and behave. If you run out of space here, you can download the Self-Monitoring Log at http://www.newharbin ger.com/51260. Alternatively, you can use a notebook to write out your observations.

In this worksheet, rate your emotions from 0 to 10, with 10 being the most intense.

Self-Monitoring Log

Situation	Emotions (Rate intensity from 0 to 10.)	Thoughts	Behavior	Physical Sensations

WHAT'S NEXT?

- *The next chapter will put your self-monitoring to use and focus on thoughts.*
- *We will explore how to question thoughts that seem unrealistic or extreme and change them, so you can think more flexibly.*
- *By practicing how to think more flexibly, you situate yourself to feel differently emotionally and behave in a way that helps you reach your goals.*

CHAPTER 6

Questioning and Changing Thoughts

- *When people are depressed or anxious, their thoughts can become unrealistic or extreme.*
- *Questioning and changing your thoughts can help you think flexibly, which can help you feel better emotionally and behave in ways that help you reach your goals.*
- *You can practice this skill by writing out your thoughts and evaluating how realistic and how helpful they are.*
- *Questioning and changing your thoughts is not about forcing yourself to think positively, it is about learning to be flexible in your thinking.*

You've done great work so far grasping many of the basic building blocks of CBT. In this chapter, we're going to build on the self-monitoring skills you practiced in chapter 5 and focus in detail on one aspect of the CBT model: your thoughts. As we've been discussing, our thoughts have tremendous influence over our emotional reactions and behaviors. And vice versa, emotions and behaviors influence how we think. For the most part, this relationship works quite well, except for when we start to treat our thoughts as facts. As we explored in the last chapter, as much as our thoughts may feel true, sometimes they're just ideas that can be extreme, unrealistic, or only part of the story. They can be subject to cognitive distortions—thinking patterns that are often misrepresentations of what's actually happening—and have the potential to amplify negative emotions and steer us in unhelpful directions.

The next step in your CBT journey is to learn how to change your thoughts, which involves identifying your thoughts (a skill you developed in chapter 5), assessing whether they are realistic and whether they really help you reach your goals, and identifying a new perspective that's more beneficial. While this sounds fairly straightforward, it can be a lot harder in practice. That's why you'll have plenty of examples and opportunities for practice in this chapter. As you'll discover, learning how to change your thoughts is a fundamental tool in CBT that can help you think more flexibly and create the emotional and behavioral changes that you need to reach the goals you set in chapter 4.

We'll first explore how to change *unrealistic* thoughts. In this first section of the chapter, you'll be provided with a number of different questions to help you reinterpret a thought or situation—especially ones that leave you feeling anxious or depressed—differently. We encourage you to try answering each of the questions and notice how this impacts how you feel about the situation or how you choose to respond to it.

The remainder of the chapter focuses on how to change *unhelpful* thoughts—meaning, the thoughts that may be or *feel* realistic but cause feelings and actions that take away from the kind of life you want to be living—to more helpful ones. There will be other questions to try out and use to come up with more helpful alternatives to these thoughts. Finally, we'll clarify common misconceptions about this strategy (spoiler alert: it isn't about positive thinking) and talk about difficulties people frequently encounter when they practice it (another spoiler alert: some thoughts can't be changed).

QUESTIONING AND CHANGING UNREALISTIC THOUGHTS

Often when people are feeling anxious or depressed their thoughts can become a little (or a lot) extreme or unrealistic—in the case of anxiety, thoughts focus on exaggerated threat, and in the case of depression, thoughts become overly self-critical. Take Jim from chapter 2. When Jim is on the cusp of having a panic attack, he has the automatic thought *If I don't control these feelings, I'm going to die.* Jim is understandably anxious and scared while he is having a panic attack—and although he might feel like he's doing to die, we know that panic attacks aren't lethal. Far from it. Panic attacks are an overextension of an otherwise normal fight-flight-freeze response, which we spoke about in chapter 2. We may also spot that Jim is engaging in catastrophizing, one of the cognitive distortions discussed in chapter 5.

Another example of unrealistic thinking comes from Victor from chapter 3, where we discussed depression. When Victor doesn't attend his grandson's soccer game on one occasion, he thinks, *I'm so lazy. I can't even get myself to a soccer game. I've let my family down.* It seems like Victor is being overly self-critical and engaging in labeling and all-or-nothing thinking, two other cognitive distortions discussed in chapter 5. Victor feels guilty and sad about not being able to go to the soccer game, but that doesn't make him lazy, nor is this necessarily as big of a disappointment to his family as he feels it is.

When you find yourself thinking automatic thoughts, or any thoughts that leave you feeling especially anxious, depressed, scared, guilty, or angry, that's a good time to put CBT to good use and change your thinking. But how exactly do we change thoughts that are unrealistic and think more flexibly? There are a number of helpful questions you can ask yourself to help identify more realistic thoughts. As you read through each, you try using the question to change a thought you've experienced recently.

You can even use some of the thoughts you wrote down in chapter 5.

What's the Evidence for and Against This Thought?

We all think how we do for good reason, in that we believe there may be *evidence* supporting how we think. Let's take Alice from chapter 2, for example, who worries that the headache she experiences may be caused by a brain tumor. She may believe this because an acquaintance with brain cancer also experienced headaches. While it's easy to look at just the evidence that supports our thinking, we also need to be able to stand back and consider information that is not entirely consistent with our first appraisal or interpretation of a situation. Alice might make note of the facts that she has no other symptoms consistent with a brain tumor, she had a recent physical exam with full blood work and no concern of cancer or illness was raised by her doctor, and the last time she had a similar headache it was after a night of poor sleep. The overall available evidence seems to be leaning toward the absence of a brain tumor.

Now, think of a situation that bothered you recently and the automatic thought you had about it. Next, try to summarize all of the evidence that supported your immediate interpretation but also consider evidence that may not have been fully supportive of your interpretation—the alternative evidence. Weigh the evidence and consider what it suggests about your original automatic thought. As an example, see Fred's attempt at evidence-gathering in response to a worry in a social situation.

Automatic Thought	What's the Evidence for This Thought?	What's the Evidence Against This Thought?
How Did This Change What I Think?		

Here's an example from Fred.

Automatic Thought	What's the Evidence for This Thought?	What's the Evidence Against This Thought?
I offended my friends when I told a joke while we were playing cards	No one laughed at the joke.	My wife thought the joke wasn't offensive. No one expressed they were upset. People seemed distracted by the game.
How Did This Change What I Think?		
Just because people didn't laugh at my joke doesn't necessarily mean I offended them. There could be other reasons why they didn't respond.		

Am I Confusing What's Possible with What's Probable?

When people feel anxious, they often tend to equate what is possible with what is probable. Sure, it's *possible* that the next time you go on vacation there could be a terrorist attack, but how many times in the past have you been on vacation *without* experiencing a terrorist attack? We would hope the majority of the time (and if not, consider changing your vacation destinations). If we're considering what is *probable* based on your experience, we would conclude your vacation will most likely be terrorist attack free. Try using the question *Am I confusing what's possible with what's probable?* to challenge another automatic thought you've had recently.

Automatic Thought	What's Possible Versus Probable in This Situation?
How Did This Change What I Think?	

This example from Jim further illustrates this tactic.

Automatic Thought	What's Possible Versus Probable in This Situation?
I will have a panic attack the next time I'm in an enclosed space.	It's possible that I might have a panic attack the next time I'm in an enclosed space, but I've also been in an elevator and grocery store several times this week without a panic attack. On the balance of probabilities, I'll be ok.
How Did This Change What I Think?	
It made me reconsider what is most likely to happen when I'm in enclosed spaces.	

What's Another Interpretation of This Situation?

It's easy to become fixed on our own understanding of a situation and assume it is the right one. But there's almost always multiple interpretations and explanations for our experiences and the behavior of others. Investigating what these other interpretations might be is a healthy thing to do, because none of us is correct all the time. For example, Jim might reinterpret his panic attack as a sign that his fight-or-flight response is working exactly as it should but is putting in overtime. He may also remind himself that panic attacks are temporary and remit on their own. He doesn't have to try to control them.

Try reinterpreting a situation or experience you had recently.

Automatic Thought	What's Another Interpretation of This Situation?
How Did This Change What I Think?	

Here's an example from Victor.

Automatic Thought	What's Another Interpretation of This Situation?
I'm a terrible grandfather because I'm not spending enough time with my grandkids.	Depression makes it very difficult to have the energy and motivation to engage with people I love. The limited time we have together is still special. I'm working on my depression in order to better my relationships with my family.
How Did This Change What I Think?	
It made me be more forgiving and less judgmental of myself.	

Will This Actually Be as Bad as I'm Assuming?

When we face uncertain or unpleasant situations, it can be easy to assume the worst and get busy catastrophizing. But we can be pleasantly surprised when things turn out better than expected. Traffic could be lighter, the medical procedure could go smoothly, or a difficult conversation with your son may help bring you closer together. That is, things can turn out better and not just exactly how you predict they will.

Experiment with challenging a thought using the question *Will this actually be as bad as I'm assuming?* below.

Automatic Thought	Will This Actually Be as Bad as I'm Assuming?
How Did This Change What I Think?	

Here is an example from Tina.

Automatic Thought	Will This Actually Be as Bad as I'm Assuming?
Babysitting my grandkids tomorrow is going to be so exhausting. I'm going to need a few days to recover.	Maybe not. They are getting a little older and can entertain themselves for a while. Perhaps I can suggest an activity that is more relaxing such as watching a movie. I could also get help from my neighbor. I may be tired at the end of the day, but I could also be energized by the visit.
How Did This Change What I Think?	
It made me consider the good and not just the bad about the visit.	

How Will I Feel About This in Six Months?

Sometimes when we experience a challenge or difficulty, it can be hard to imagine how you'll ever get over it or through it. On the other hand, we can probably all think back to a negative life event that, with the passage of time, wasn't the end of the world, even if it was difficult at times. And the minor negative experiences? We often forget those altogether. Do you remember all the buses or trains that you've missed?

Even for more significant negative life experiences, we tend to underestimate how with time, we can adapt to negative events and even create meaning from what happened. There may even be positives that come out of difficult experiences. Let's take breaking your arm, for example. There's no denying this can be painful and a downright nuisance when you realize what limitations it imposes (try using a can opener with one hand). With time, however, you will likely recover, although not always perfectly, and you may even have a renewed appreciation for your arm and its many capabilities (beyond just using can openers). Additionally, you may be grateful for people who came together to support you while you were recovering. The experience could also come with unexpected upsides, such as more support from others, time to rest, and helpful health care providers. It's useful to remind ourselves that with time, we can adapt to and feel differently about negative events.

Choose a challenge or difficulty you've experienced and answer the question *How will I feel about this in six months?* below.

Automatic Thought	How Will I Feel About This in Six Months?
How Did This Change What I think?	

Here is an example from Victor.

Automatic Thought	How Will I Feel About This in Six Months?
I shouldn't have lost my temper with my daughter. I'm a terrible communicator. How will she ever forgive me?	This will likely be less important in six months. I will feel better after I apologize. I can learn how to communicate better with her in the future.
How Did This Change What I think?	
It helped me keep the conversation in perspective.	

What Would I Tell a Loved One Who Was Having This Thought?

Do you ever pay attention to the advice you give to others and think, *Wow, that was very sensible. If only I could take my own advice.* You're not alone. Most of us tend to be more realistic and understanding when giving advice to loved ones—but when it comes to giving advice to ourselves, that often just goes right out the window. We tend to be more critical, unforgiving, and unrealistic.

Write down a thought you've had that seems unrealistic or overly critical and identify what you would tell a loved one who was thinking the same thing. Try to turn that advice inward.

Automatic Thought	What Would I Tell a Loved One Who Was Having This Thought?
How Did This Change What I Think?	

Here is an example of how this works for Fred.

Automatic Thought	What Would I Tell a Loved One Who Was Having This Thought?
How embarrassing to stumble on my words in the meeting. People must have thought I was a bumbling old man.	No one speaks perfectly all the time. It may not have been as noticeable as I think. People are usually paying attention to themselves more than others. You can't control what they think anyway.
How Did This Change What I Think?	
It helped me be more accepting of being imperfect.	

QUESTIONING AND CHANGING UNHELPFUL THOUGHTS

Up to this point, we've focused on thoughts that we know or suspect to be unrealistic in some way. You might also notice yourself having thoughts while feeling anxious or depressed that you believe to be realistic. For example, Victor often has the thought *I'm wasting my retirement because I'm so depressed*—and he thinks it's a true statement. Now what? Well, this thought might be a realistic one in Victor's mind, but whether it's a helpful thought is another issue. Let's come back to the idea that our thoughts impact our emotions and behavior. How might this thought impact Victor? He's likely to feel guilty, angry with himself, and potentially more depressed. It's hard to imagine how this will help him take actions to feel better emotionally, such as getting physical exercise, playing guitar, or spending time with his family—the actions that might even help him *disprove* his thought and deal with the emotion that drives it. In other words, the thought *I'm wasting my retirement because I'm so depressed* is unhelpful. It doesn't help Victor feel better emotionally or prompt him to take actions that are in service of his goals. It's important to be able to recognize thoughts you have that might be—or just feel—realistic but aren't helpful, so you can evaluate them and change them, too.

Unhelpful thoughts can be changed using several different questions that we'll elaborate on below.

If Someone Spoke to Me How I Spoke to Myself, How Would I Feel or Behave? Would this Help Me Reach My Goals?

Imagine you have an appointment with your doctor to discuss recent health changes, and instead of a professional discussion your doctor says, "You again! There's always something wrong with you. Can't you do anything right to improve your health?" How would you react? You might storm out of the office and promptly launch a complaint—and you'd be justified in doing that. You might also feel belittled, ashamed, sad, or demoralized. You certainly wouldn't want to see the doctor again or follow any medical instructions they gave you.

Similarly, when you speak to yourself in ways that are demeaning or critical, not only are you creating emotional pain, but you're also not doing what works to create behavior change. When you speak to yourself in ways that are encouraging, supportive, and understanding, you're more likely to feel better emotionally and take positive steps toward your goals. Think about being a supportive coach to yourself as opposed to an army drill sergeant.

Try this strategy out below by choosing a thought and answering the question about how you would speak to someone else in a similar situation.

Automatic Thought	If Someone Spoke to Me How I Spoke to Myself, How Would I Feel or Behave? Would This Help Me Reach My Goals?
How Did This Change What I Think?	

Consider how Jim used this strategy to think in a more helpful way.

Automatic Thought	If Someone Spoke to Me How I Spoke to Myself, How Would I Feel or Behave? Would This Help Me Reach My Goals?
I'm weak because I can't control my panic attacks.	I would feel ashamed if someone spoke to me this way. I would want to give up trying. Instead, I can remind myself that no one chooses to have panic attacks. Everyone has their own struggles. Seeking help makes me a stronger person.
How Did This Change What I Think?	
It made me more understanding and compassionate toward myself.	

What Are the Pros and Cons of Thinking this Way?

There may be many upsides to how you think (it's certainly gotten you this far in life), but there can also be plenty of downsides. For example, you might assume that worrying will help you prepare for worst case-scenarios (such as thinking that worrying about a car accident would help you be better prepared for one). A pro of thinking this way is if a worst-case scenario happens, you will have what you need to deal with the situation. Crisis averted. The cons of thinking this way are that worst-case scenarios don't consistently happen, which means that you'll often spend considerable time and energy thinking and preparing for things that don't happen. What's more, if you're constantly thinking about and preparing for catastrophes, you'll likely also feel anxious a good portion of the time. Finally, all that worrying may make it difficult to be in the present moment. All in all, the cons of worrying to prepare for catastrophes might outweigh the pros.

Assessing both the pros and cons of a thought can help you assess whether a thought that seems helpful is actually helping or harming you. Give this a shot below with a recent automatic thought you had.

Automatic Thought	What Are the Pros of Thinking This Way?	What Are the Cons of Thinking This Way?

How Did This Change What I Think?

Here is an example from Tina.

Automatic Thought	What Are the Pros of Thinking This Way?	What Are the Cons of Thinking This Way?
If I worry, I'll be less surprised and upset when bad things happen.	I feel more in control.	I can't anticipate every bad thing that could possibly happen. I feel more anxious when I do. I can't guarantee that I won't feel any emotional pain when bad things happen. There's a chance I may feel just as bad.

How Did This Change What I Think?

It made me reevaluate whether worrying does actually make me more prepared to deal with bad things.

What Would Life Be Like If I Let This Thought Go?

Our thoughts have tremendous power in shaping how we feel, the choices we make, and how we go about our everyday lives. Unhelpful thoughts can loom over us, overshadowing other important aspects of our daily lives, limit our choices, and take away from the pleasure or satisfaction we might otherwise derive from life. If you were able to release a thought and let it go, how would that change your life? Maybe you would feel lighter, confident, more motivated, at peace, or content. Perhaps you'd take more chances, come out of your shell, and be able to connect better with the people in your life. Maybe you'd make lifestyle changes like improving your diet, getting more exercise, or changing your housing situation. Considering how releasing a thought would change your life can help you realize how it may be limiting you in important ways.

Practice reflecting on this below.

Automatic Thought	What Would Life Be Like If I Let This Thought Go?
How Did This Change What I Think?	

As an example, here's what Alice wrote for her health worries.

Automatic Thought	What Would Life Be Like If I Let This Thought Go?
I must find out what this headache is. I should be able explain any physical sensation.	I would be able to have aches and pains without spiraling into anxiety. I would be able to accept what is out of my control. I would be able to move on with my life and do more of what I enjoy doing.
How Did This Change What I Think?	
It made me let go of the need to explain all my physical sensations.	

You've just worked your way through nine different questions to help you change your way of thinking. To reiterate, these questions are introduced to guide you to identify thinking patterns that are likely to be present whenever you are feeling shifts in negative mood states.

Often when people are experiencing anxiety or depression, their thoughts tend to spiral in ways that are extreme or counterproductive. Taking the time to write out your thoughts and go through any of the above questions can help you to come to a new understanding or interpretation of a situation. That can, in turn, help shift how you're feeling and how you're behaving.

COMMON QUESTIONS AND CONCERNS

Now's let get ahead of some possible problems by addressing common questions and concerns people have when they're attempting to change their thinking.

Do I Really Need to Write Things Down?

It can be tempting to breeze through these questions and try to answer them in your head. We would strongly encourage you to, at least at first, write out your thoughts and responses to the questions above. Why is this so important? First, the act of writing our thought down can help us develop a different perspective on that thought and be better able to let it go. Seeing a thought down on paper can also allow us to be more objective about it. So, yes, write it down. You can use shortcuts, including making more abbreviated notes, if that makes the task more accessible for you.

Is This About Trying to Think Positively?

It can be tempting to read all about changing your thinking and assume that the goal here is to turn your negative thoughts into positive ones. But that couldn't be further from the actual intent. Positive thinking can be just as problematic as negative thinking. If you thought everything was always going to work out perfectly, you'd often be ill prepared or disappointed. If you ignored your mistakes, you'd never learn from them. If you just wished for positive changes in your life, you could be neglecting opportunities to make different choices. The goal of changing your thinking is ultimately to be more flexible and realistic, not necessarily more positive.

I Don't Feel Better After I've Changed My Thinking. Am I Doing It Right?

When some people attempt to change their thinking, they may experience changes in their emotions: an easing of anxiety, a boost of mood, alleviation of anger, or a decrease of guilt or shame. But other people might not experience those emotional changes, and that's ok. Even if you don't feel an improvement in how you feel emotionally, when you shift your thinking, there is still value in using this tool.

Imagine going on a hike in the woods only to find yourself going down the same path over and over again. Over time, the path will become well-worn, and the treads in the ground are going to get deeper and deeper. If you decide to take a different path, it'll take some time for that path to be as well-worn as the original one you're used to taking. In our brains, the more certain thoughts are rehearsed, the more habitual they become and the harder it can be to break out of these patterns of thinking. Challenging our thoughts and learning to think flexibly allows us to create new mental habits, so we're not limited by our negative ways of thinking. That is valuable in and of itself, even if your emotions don't immediately show it.

I Keep on Coming Back to the Same Thoughts Over and Over. How Do I Stop Doing This?

Repetitive thinking is very common when you struggle with depression and anxiety. It can take three different forms:

- *Rumination* involves repetitive thinking about one's negative mood state *(I'm so depressed)* or life circumstances *(Why did my marriage end?)*. This is most common when people are depressed.
- *Worry* involves repetitive thinking about negative outcomes that may happen in the future *(What if I develop dementia?)*. This is most common for people with anxiety disorders.
- *Doubt* involves repetitive questioning in uncertain circumstances *(Did I remember to lock the door?)*. This occurs frequently in anxiety disorders and other conditions such as obsessive-compulsive disorder.

Our brains like certainty (or the perception of it), and we can often fall into repetitive thinking as a way to understand or control things that are distressing to us. Repetitive thinking has few benefits, however, because it doesn't usually generate the insights or emotional relief we're hoping for. When you notice that you're engaging in repetitive thinking, it is helpful to ask yourself a few questions:

- Am I thinking about a situation that is actually happening or will happen soon (versus a past situation or a hypothetical one in the future)?
- Is there anything I can do about the situation I'm thinking about?
- Will repetitive thinking bring me additional clarity on the situation?
- Is repetitive thinking about how I feel making me feel better?

If you answered no to any of the above questions, you've identified that your repetitive thinking is unhelpful and not getting you anywhere (except perhaps feeling more depressed or anxious). If that's case, we would recommend a strategy that psychologist Robert Leahy discussed in his book *The Worry Cure* (2006). Tell yourself that you can come back to repetitive thinking later in the day and even pick a time to do so (for example, 6p.m.). Then, let the thought you're having go, with the knowledge that you can come back to it at your designated worry time. The point is to practice deferring your engagement in your thoughts. It's like kicking a can down the sidewalk, knowing that you can catch up to it later.

This is *not* the same thing as telling yourself to *stop thinking*. This will likely make you engage in even more repetitive thinking. Rather, this is about giving yourself permission to think, but putting that off until later in the day at a predetermined time. Afterall, what's going to change about the situation if you think about it now or later? Because it's repetitive thinking, absolutely nothing. This way, you can bring your focus in this moment back to whatever it is you're actually doing.

Best-case scenario, your repetitive thinking time comes and goes, and you realize that you've forgotten about it. Again, the point isn't necessarily to overthink but to practice putting off the repetitive thinking you're feeling compelled to do. If you do decide to come back to the thoughts at your dedicated time, we recommend that you use the time to challenge those thoughts, using any of the questions highlighted in this chapter, and try to change them.

Additionally, set some parameters for how long you engage in your repetitive thinking time, for example, twenty minutes of writing out thoughts and challenging them. This can help contain how much time and energy you direct toward your thoughts.

The Thought I've Written Down Is a Fact. I Can't Change It. Now What?

Not all of our thoughts are unrealistic, extreme, or unhelpful. Sometimes you'll have a thought that is just a fact. *I have cognitive impairment, I don't live in the same city as my immediate family,* or *I will need hip replacement surgery* are all examples of facts. Dealing with the realities of aging can be challenging and upsetting, especially when there's so much that we can't control. In the chapters to come, we'll discuss how we can better practice the skill of acceptance when we're faced with situations that we can't change and aren't happy about. Chapter 8 will cover how to become a better problem-solver, which is often needed as we decide what to do in a difficult situation. Keep reading to learn more about these concepts and adding to your CBT tool kit.

In sum, those are the ins and outs of questioning and changing your thinking, a fundamental CBT tool to help you think more flexibly. Like any skill, it takes practice until it becomes more habitual. The exercise in the section "Putting CBT into Practice" later in the chapter is designed to help with that. Be patient with yourself as you attempt to think differently. Changing how you think takes time, especially with thoughts that may have been present for a long time. However, we can promise that your efforts will be worthwhile because a changed mind is a changed life. And that's a helpful thought if there ever was one.

TAKE-HOME POINTS

- *The tool of questioning and changing your thinking can help you change how you feel and how you behave.*
- *Writing down your thoughts and using different questions to assess how realistic or helpful a thought is can help you identify a new perspective.*
- *Changing your thoughts is not about thinking positively, it is about thinking flexibly.*
- *Repetitive negative thinking, can be reduced by setting up a time to ruminate and practicing deferring your worrying until that time.*
- *Certain thoughts can't be changed. These are better dealt with through practicing acceptance and /or engaging in problem-solving, which we will discuss in later chapters.*

PUTTING CBT INTO PRACTICE

Continue practicing questioning and changing your thoughts this week. Once a day, try to identify a thought and use any of the questions below to help assess whether the thought is realistic or helpful and identify a new perspective. (You can download Questions to Change

Unrealistic Thoughts and Questions to Change Unhelpful Thoughts in handout form at http://www.newharbinger.com/51260.)

Questions to Change Unrealistic & Unhelpful Thoughts

Questions to Change Unrealistic Thoughts
• What's the evidence for and against this thought?
• Am I confusing what's possible with what's probable?
• What's another interpretation of this situation?
• Will this actually be as bad as I'm assuming?
• How will I feel about this in six months?
• What would I tell a loved one who was having this thought?

Questions to Change Unhelpful Thoughts
• If someone spoke to me how I spoke to myself, how would I feel or behave? Would this help me reach my goals?
• What are the pros and cons of thinking this way?
• What would life be like if I let this thought go?

To further explore some of your automatic thoughts, note them in the Changing Automatic Thoughts Worksheet below along with the question(s) you used and responses to the question. (You can download this worksheet at http://www.newharbinger.com/51260.) You can also use a notebook for this exercise. The more you practice this skill, the more automatic it will become and the more flexible you will be in your thinking. This will set you up to help reach the goals you identified in chapter 4.

Changing Automatic Thoughts Worksheet

Automatic Thought	Question(s) Used	Response

WHAT'S NEXT?

- *The next chapter will focus on changing behaviors that go hand-in-hand with depression (such as inactivity, withdrawal, or isolation) and anxiety (such as avoidance or overdoing).*
- *We will introduce the idea of exposure therapy and discuss how this can help reduce your fears.*
- *We will introduce the idea of behavioral activation and discuss how this can help boost your mood.*

CHAPTER 7

Changing Your Behavior

- *Exposure therapy is an effective behavioral intervention for anxiety that involves repeatedly facing feared situations, thoughts, emotions, or physical sensations.*
- *The repetitive facing of fears leads to a reduction of anxiety and increased confidence to face and manage situations that have in the past prompted distress and avoidance.*
- *Behavioral activation is a powerful behavioral intervention for depression. It involves daily engagement in mood-boosting activities that provide a sense of pleasure, mastery, and/or meaning.*

You've already come far in your CBT journey. Most recently, you've learned and applied skills to help to you think differently when you notice your thoughts becoming unrealistic or unhelpful, which is a common side effect of anxiety and depression. Thinking differently, as important as it is, is only part of the solution to feeling better, however. Changing behaviors that maintain anxiety or depression is a powerful step that will have you both feeling better and more confident in your abilities to cope with difficult emotions in late life.

In previous chapters, we've highlighted how behaviors such as avoidance (for example, avoidance of situations, tasks, or social contact; procrastination; or distraction) and overdoing (for example, list-making, overplanning, reassurance seeking, or researching) tend to maintain anxiety and depression over the long term even though they can reduce distress in the moment. These are the behaviors we'll be targeting in this chapter. You might be wondering how exactly CBT helps people change these behaviors. As you read this chapter, you might notice that the two main behavioral interventions for anxiety and depression build on truisms that you have likely heard. You've probably heard of the idea of facing your fear, which is at the heart of *exposure therapy*, a behavioral intervention for anxiety we'll be discussing first. Second, you're likely no stranger to the ideas that slow and steady wins the race and that objects in motion stay in motion, which are integral to *behavioral activation* for depression, which we'll be discussing in the second half of this chapter. In many ways CBT builds on ideas and strategies that you may be already familiar with and expands on them based on decades of scientific research on behavior change. We can feel your eagerness to get going, so let's turn first to a behavioral strategy for reducing anxiety: exposure therapy.

REDUCING ANXIETY THROUGH EXPOSURE THERAPY

Think back to your childhood for a moment and try to remember something you were afraid of that you aren't anymore. Let's take a fear of the dark, for example. How did you become less afraid of the dark? We're guessing that you didn't sleep with all the lights on until you were old enough to know better. Perhaps your parents left a hallway light on at first or gave you a nightlight in your room until you felt more comfortable in total darkness. How long did it take to reduce your fear of the dark? A single night or at least several nights by yourself in the dark? Your answers to these questions illustrate the principles of exposure therapy. Exposure therapy is defined most simply as the exposure to a feared situation, thought, or emotion, fully and repeatedly, which allows us to learn over time that what we expected would happen either didn't occur or isn't as bad as we expect. Let's explore the key components of this definition further.

Facing Fears Fully

The first important component of exposure therapy is facing your fears fully. This means being fully attentive to the feared situation, emotion, or thought as opposed to trying to distract yourself from it or not being entirely present. If Fred is trying to reduce his fear of meeting new people by attending a social event at his church, for example, it wouldn't be helpful for him to spend time at the social event reading the newspaper. Likewise, if Jim is trying to reduce his fear of panicking while in the grocery store, exposure therapy would fall flat if he tried to distract himself at the grocery store by talking on the phone.

Facing fears fully also means to confront a *variety* of situations, thoughts, or emotions associated with your fears. Tina tends to feel more anxious in uncertain situations (for example, taking care of her grandkids, having enough money for retirement, and going to new restaurants) and tends to overplan or prepare as a result. Her exposures should target a wide range of uncertain situations and not just one. For example, she might have her grandkids over and not make a plan for their afternoon, limit the amount of time she spends reviewing her finances, and try a new restaurant she's never tried before without looking at the menu beforehand. This will help Tina's anxiety reduce across different contexts and not just one, such as taking care of her grandkids.

Facing Fears Repeatedly

The second important component of exposure therapy is facing fears repeatedly. Not only do we need to face fears fully and across contexts, but we also often need to have these experiences repeatedly. From decades of scientific research on everything from rats to chimpanzees to humans, we know that repeated exposure to our fears results in fear reduction over time. Your first time facing a fear will likely feel uncomfortable, but as you experience this repeatedly, your fear will reduce each time. Figure 11 illustrates what to expect in repeating exposures: typically, your anxiety will peak in intensity during an exposure and then reduce. On subsequent exposures, your anxiety will not peak as high and then reduce faster. Fear typically decreases over repeated exposures because of the new learning that happens during exposures. We'll speak to that next.

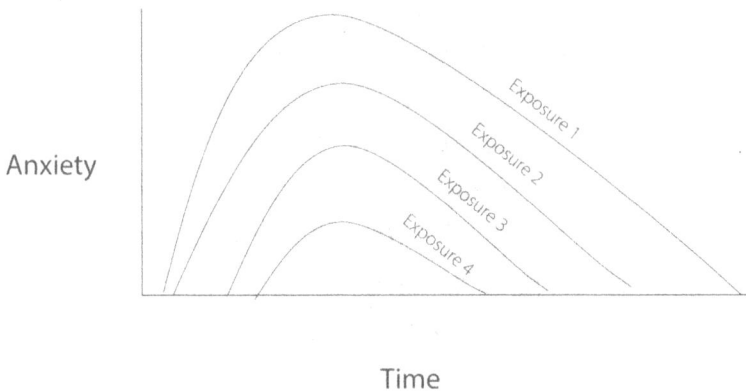

Figure 11. During an exposure, your anxiety will peak in intensity and then reduce. On subsequent exposures, your anxiety will not peak as high and then reduce faster.

Facing Fears to Learn Something Valuable

The third most important component of exposure therapy is that these experiences set you up to learn something important about your fears. People usually think that whatever they fear, whether it's having a medical examination, public speaking, or having a disagreement with a friend, will end up terribly (remember the cognitive distortion *catastrophizing* from chapter 5?), and they have little confidence in their ability to cope with what happens. Effective exposures will help people violate these assumptions in a powerful way. Take Fred, for example, who assumes that if he doesn't speak in a smart and articulate way around others, this will ultimately result in rejection. A powerful form of exposure for him could be to *purposely* slip up on his words or misspeak when talking to others in order to see what actually happens (for example, do people walk away immediately or laugh in his face?), and even if it is uncomfortable or awkward, is that the end of the world? Effective exposures usually demonstrate to us that we overpredicted how bad something would be and that we are more capable of coping than we give ourselves credit for.

In preparation for your exposure therapy, take a moment to reflect on what you predict will happen in scenarios that you fear and write those down below. You can review examples from Tina and Jim below.

My predictions: _____

_____

Tina's predictions: (1) If I don't have everything planned out for my grandkids visit, they will have a terrible time and I will feel unbearably stressed. (2) If I don't review my financial situation every day for an hour, then I will lose control of my finances and overspend.

Jim's predictions: (1) If I drink two cups of coffee and do physical exercise, I will cause a panic attack and pass out. (2) If I don't leave the movie theater when I feel anxious, my anxiety will continue to escalate until I have a heart attack.

TYPES OF EXPOSURE

With a grasp of the principles of exposure therapy, let's review different types of exposure that people can engage in depending on the nature of their fear.

Situational Exposures

The first type of exposure is *situational* wherein people confront situations or things that they are afraid of, such as highway driving, going to the dentist, saying no to a request from someone, having an unproductive day, having a medical procedure, preparing a will, going to a crowded place, being underprepared for a meeting, or going on public transit. If your fear is one that permits you to face it in this fashion, then situational exposures are best for you.

Imaginal Exposures

There are some fears that we can't either safely or logistically expose people to repeatedly such as a fear of death/dying, air travel, serious disease or illness, or harm to loved ones. For these fears, *imaginal* exposures are better suited. For this type of exposure, people write out a narrative of the scenario they're worried about with as much detail as possible. For example, if Alice is worried about dying of cancer, she might write out a narrative account of being diagnosed, telling loved ones, going through chemotherapy and radiation treatment, her emotional reactions, her physical symptoms and experience, and eventual decline until death. The narrative should evoke a strong emotional reaction for the reader. Individuals would then read this narrative repeatedly until their emotional reaction to this scenario changes and the thought itself of the feared scenario doesn't elicit debilitating anxiety. People might also record themselves reading the narrative out loud and listen to it repeatedly instead. If imaginal exposure seems somewhat torturous, you wouldn't be the only one to think so. Remember the point of exposures is not just to be uncomfortable for the sake of being uncomfortable. It is in order to learn that you *can* cope with the discomfort you experience and that it will decrease with time. It's discomfort in service of greater acceptance and inner peace.

Interoceptive Exposures

One final form of exposure to consider is called *interoceptive* exposure. Interoceptive means produced within the body. This form is exposure is suited for people who feel anxious about certain physical sensations, such as increased heart rate, changes in breathing, dizziness or lightheadedness, or hot flashes. This is common for people who experience panic attacks. For this form of exposure, people intentionally produce physical sensations that might mimic a panic attack, such as running up a flight of stairs or hyperventilating for thirty seconds. A list of different interoceptive exposures is provided below. This might sound (or look) a little silly, but it is incredibly effective at reducing people's fear of physical sensations associated with panic. With repeated exposure, people learn that these sensations are uncomfortable but not dangerous and that our bodies work to bring us back to normal without any conscious effort to do so. If you think interoceptive exposures are right for you, speak to your medical doctor first to ensure that it is medically safe to do so. There are some medical conditions that older adults may experience wherein interoceptive exposures may be contraindicated, such as certain cardiac conditions, epilepsy, or asthma. Further, if you are at risk of falling, you may want to conduct certain exposures (for example, inducing dizziness) in the presence of another person or avoid them altogether.

Feared Physical Sensation	Interoceptive Exposure
Rapid heart rate	• Run on the spot for one minute. • Run up a flight of stairs.
Dizziness/ light-headedness	• Spin around in circles while sitting in chair for thirty seconds. • Move head from side to side for thirty seconds. • Hyperventilate for sixty seconds.
Shortness of breath	• Hyperventilate for sixty seconds. • Breathe through a straw and plug nose for sixty seconds. • Hold breath for thirty seconds.
Hot flashes/ sweating	• Sit in warm room with a sweater or other layers on.
Unreality	• Stare at hand for three minutes. • Look at self in mirror for five minutes. • Stare at a light for one minute and then try to read something.

From our description of the different types of exposures, make a note of which form of exposure you think would be most beneficial for your fears. Go back to the predictions you wrote down above to help you identify which fears you're facing and with what form of exposure. You can see Tina and Jim's examples below.

	Situational Exposures	Imaginal Exposures	Interoceptive Exposure
My predictions:			

Here are examples from Tina and Jim.

	Situational Exposures	Imaginal Exposures	Interoceptive Exposure
Tina's predictions:			
If I don't have everything planned out for my grandkids visit, they will have a terrible time and I will feel unbearably stressed.	X		
If I don't review my financial situation every day for an hour, then I will lose control of my finances and overspend.	X		
Jim's predictions:			
If I drink two cups of coffee and do physical exercise, I will cause a panic attack and pass out.	X	X	X
If I don't leave the movie theater when I feel anxious, my anxiety will continue to escalate until I have a heart attack.	X		

HOW TO DO EXPOSURES

Now let's talk about the nuts and bolts of doing exposures and review step-by-step guidelines for facing your fears.

Exposures: Step 1

Create a list of your feared situations, thoughts, or physical sensations and order them from least challenging to most challenging. Try to generate a variety of different entries on your exposure step ladder that will differ not only in intensity (that is, minimal anxiety to the most anxiety) but also in nature of the task and even location, if applicable. It can be helpful to rate the difficulty level of each, with 10 being the most difficult and 1 being the least difficult. Your best estimate is sufficient.

See examples for Tina and Jim below.

Tina's Exposures	Difficulty *Rate on a scale of 1 to 10.*
Have all grandkids over for sleepover without a schedule	9–10
Have two grandkids over for full day without a schedule	7–8
Have one grandchild over for an afternoon with only one planned activity	5–6
Make a small impulse purchase (<$20)	3–4
Review finances for fifteen minutes a day instead of one hour	1–2

Jim's Exposures	Difficulty *Rate on a scale of 1 to 10.*
Hyperventilate for thirty seconds in movie theater	9–10
Review written script of having heart attack in movie theater	7–8
Drink two cups of coffee and run up flight of stairs	5–6
Drink one cup of coffee and run on the spot for one minute	3–4
Drink one cup of coffee and go for fifteen-minute walk	1–2

Now it's your turn. For this worksheet, rate difficulty on a scale of 1 to 10, with 10 being the most difficult and 1 being the least difficult.

My Exposures	Difficulty *Rate on a scale of 1 to 10.*
	9–10
	7–8
	5–6
	3–4
	1–2

Exposures: Step 2

Decide when and how often you'll be doing your exposures and commit to it. The ideal frequency of doing exposures is daily. That might seem like a lot, but it's important to remember that we tend to learn best when we practice often and in close succession. If you were trying to learn how to ride a bike and only practiced once a week, it would take a longer amount of time to become skilled than if you rode every day. Think ahead and plan out which exposures you will be attempting and on what day. Make sure you have what you need to complete the exposure. For example, if Fred wants to do an exposure where he makes a mistake in front of others, he'll need to plan to have friends over and purposely make a blunder (for example, use the coffee maker incorrectly).

Exposures: Step 3

Track your experiences during the exposure. There are two important things to track during an exposure and the first involves your anxiety intensity. It is helpful to rate your anxiety on a scale of 10 during your exposure, with 10 being the most intense and 0 being no anxiety. Make note of how intense your anxiety becomes during the exposure (for example, 8) and then rerate your anxiety upon completion of the exposure (for example, 4). What is most important is seeing how your *peak* anxiety rating changes across repeated exposures as opposed to seeing it reduce within a single exposure. Tracking your anxiety helps identify that it's decreasing over repeated exposures, signaling that you're learning from your exposures.

Second, it's important to track the outcome of your exposure. Remember that we're trying to test out the predictions to see if your feared scenario is as bad as you thought it would be and whether you're capable of making it through the discomfort. At the end of the exposure, make note of what happened as objectively as possible and what you learned from the exposure. We'll include an example of this tracking below.

Exposures: Step 4

Minimize the use of any safety behaviors during an exposure. Safety behaviors are subtle (or sometimes not-so-subtle) things that people engage in to help themselves feel better during an exposure. They can be varied and depend on the nature of someone's fear. Examples of safety behaviors are included below. Go through and try to identify which, if any, of these you might be inclined to do during an exposure.

Examples of Safety Behaviors

	✓
Relying on a "safe" person	
Checking your body (for example, blood pressure or heart rate)	
Sitting near an exit	
Trying to control breathing	
Seeking reassurance	
Using protective barriers (for example, tissue or clothing) when touching public surfaces	
Keeping antianxiety medication on hand	
Mentally rehearsing before speaking	
Avoiding eye contact	
Keeping your replies short	
Wearing clothing that hides what you consider problem areas	
Doing online research	
Other: _____	

Safety behaviors are problematic because they interfere with learning what we need to during an exposure to help us reduce our anxiety. If Jim is doing his exposure involving hyperventilating in a movie theater but then tries to control his breathing after doing so, this limits him from learning that his body will bring him back to normal *without* him trying to control his breath. This safety behavior also reinforces the inaccurate assumption that the physical sensations produced during and following hyperventilation are dangerous and need to be stopped. This is all the more reason to avoid or restrict the use of safety behaviors as much as possible during exposures.

Summary: Exposure Therapy Steps

To summarize, the four steps of exposure therapy are:

1. Create a list of your feared situations, thoughts, or physical sensations and order them from least challenging to most challenging. (Consult this list to pick which exposures to work on.)
2. Make a plan for when and how often you'll be doing your exposures and commit to it.
3. Track your experiences during the exposure.
4. Minimize the use of any safety behaviors during an exposure.

And there you have it. The fundamentals of exposure therapy to help you reduce your anxiety. If you're feeling intimidated or overwhelmed at the thoughts of facing your fears, that is perfectly understandable. Most older adults feel nervous before starting exposures and are reluctant to do so. Know that the anticipation of exposures can often be worse than the actual exposures themselves. Once people get into the habit of facing their fears, many find that it's not as bad as they expected.

We have captured the four steps for exposure therapy in the Exposure Therapy

Tracking Form that will also help you track your progress while doing exposures. We included a blank form in the "Putting CBT into Practice" section later in the chapter to help guide your exposures. You can download additional copies of this form at http://www.newharbinger.com/51 260.

You may find that engaging in self-directed exposures on a regular basis is doable for you and helps you reach your goals. Other people find exposures to be too challenging to do on their own and may require the assistance of a mental health professional. If that is your experience, you're not alone. Facing your fears can be very challenging and sometimes help from a qualified professional is needed to help you benefit from exposures as much as you can. Don't hesitate to reach out for help if needed.

This example shows how Tina completed her exposures. For this worksheet, anxiety is rated on a scale of 0 to 10, with 10 being the most intense and 0 being no anxiety.

Exposure Therapy Tracking Form

Tina's Exposures	Date	Peak Anxiety Rate on a scale of 0 to 10.	End Anxiety Rate on a scale of 0 to 10.	What I Learned	Safety Behaviors I Avoided
Review finances for fifteen minutes a day instead of one hour	Monday	4	2	It wasn't as hard as I expected.	Seeking reassurance from husband
Review finances for fifteen minutes a day instead of one hour	Tuesday	3	1	Reviewing less doesn't make me lose control of my finances.	Seeking reassurance from husband
Review finances for ten minutes a day instead of one hour	Wednesday	1	0	I feel less anxious as I review less.	Seeking reassurance from husband
Have one grandchild over for an afternoon with only one planned activity	Thursday	6	3	We can fill the time even if I don't plan everything.	Researching activities to do with kids. Calling daughter
Have one grandchild over for an afternoon with no planned activities	Friday	4	2	Leaving things unplanned led to spontaneous, fun playtime. It is less tiring to leave things unplanned.	Researching activities to do with kids. Calling daughter

REDUCING DEPRESSION THROUGH BEHAVIORAL ACTIVATION

Now let's turn to learning about behavioral activation, a powerful tool for improving your mood. Let's first review the vicious cycle of depression and inactivity that can often occur with this condition. When people are struggling with depression, daily tasks, such as taking the dog for a walk or making a meal, can feel like mountains to climb. It can be difficult to summon the motivation to do these things. These tasks are easily overlooked as potential mood boosters, but when people aren't engaged in them, they tend to feel even more depressed. This is in part because they missed out on something enjoyable and putting a deposit in their "mood bank account" but also due to negative self-talk that emerges as a result of inactivity (for example, *I can't even make myself a meal, I'm so incapable,* or *I'm letting others down.*). This sets people up to perpetuate a vicious cycle of activity disengagement, as shown in figure 12. As the law of physics goes, objects at rest stay at rest (and in this case, depressed).

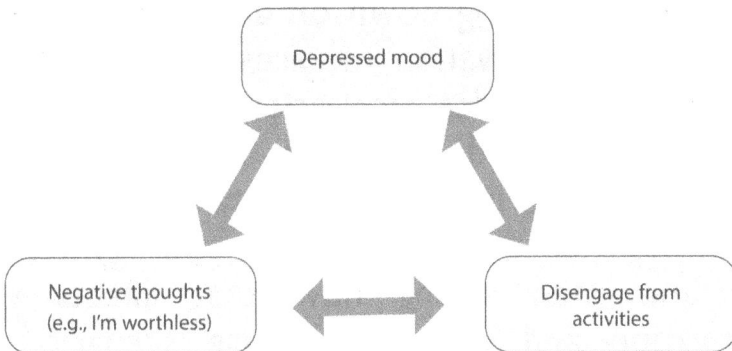

Figure 12. Activity disengagement cycle.

With behavioral activation, the goal is to reengage in activities that have gone by the wayside during an episode of depression and to break the cycle of negative thoughts and depressed mood. The idea is to *behave your way into feeling and thinking differently.* You may be thinking, *That sounds simple enough, but how on earth am I supposed to reengage in what feels good when depression has sapped all my motivation?* It's a great question that is best answered by shifting your paradigm about motivation.

We commonly assume that motivation is needed before you take an action, for example, *Once I feel like exercising, I'll start going to the gym again.* The downside of waiting for motivation to arrive is that you may be waiting forever and never actually take the step you want or need to. This also neglects the idea that motivation can occur as the *result of* taking action, for example, *As I go back to the gym, I will feel more motivated to exercise.* This is especially the case when you're feeling down or depressed. Engaging in behavioral activation requires you to consider that action precedes motivation and not just the other way around, as shown in figure 13. The important thing is to focus on taking action in a *small* way (for example, putting your gym shoes on) and then seeing how that affects your motivation and mood. Best-case scenario, you start to notice a shift in your motivation and mood and decide to head over to the gym. Even if there isn't, at least you haven't made your mood worse by remaining inactive and you've taken a step toward something important. That is just as valuable.

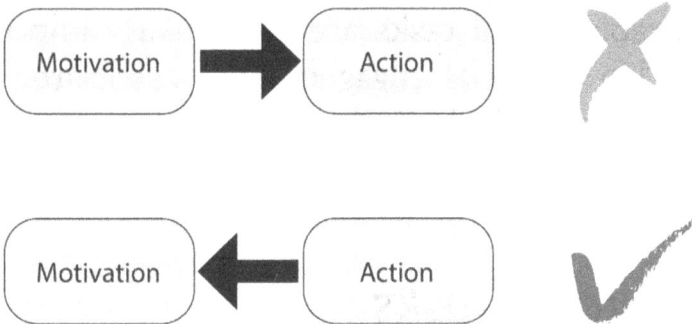

Figure 13. Relationship between action and motivation.

Before we outline a step-by-step guide for engaging in behavioral activation, there is an important distinction to make between different types of mood-boosting activities. Have you ever noticed that there are different types of "feeling good"? The mood boost you get from watching your favorite movie is likely different from the one you get from finally reorganizing your bedroom closet or going to a church service. CBT makes the distinction between tasks that provide *pleasure, mastery,* or *meaning.*

Pleasurable tasks are those that we engage in because they just feel good intrinsically. They can include a variety of different things such as hobbies (for example, gardening, traveling, arts and crafts, board games, reading, or photography), sensory pleasures (for example, enjoying a meal, listening to music, smelling something pleasurable, taking a bath, or going for a swim), and social activities (for example, spending time with family or friends, reminiscing with a friend, going to social gatherings, or engaging with animals). Pleasurable social tasks are particularly important in late life as social engagement is associated with a whole host of physical, cognitive, and emotional benefits. List a few of your pleasurable tasks below.

Pleasurable tasks

- _____
- _____
- _____
- _____

Mastery tasks, on the other hand, are mood boosting because they typically involve an accomplishment or developing a skill. They may not always feel as great in the moment as pleasurable tasks, but usually after we engage in mastery tasks, we feel better for it. Examples of mastery tasks can include doing your taxes, cleaning up or organizing around the home, attending an appointment, learning a new language, practicing a musical instrument, attending a course or workshop, going grocery shopping, and learning how to do something on the computer. They can be smaller- or larger-scale accomplishments or skills. List a few of your mastery tasks below.

Mastery tasks

- _____

- _____
- _____
- _____

Finally, meaningful tasks feel good because they involve us doing something that is consistent with our values. For example, if someone values community involvement, a meaningful task might involve attending a city council meeting to speak out about an important issue to them. Someone else might derive meaning from spirituality or religious involvement and as such, going to church is a mood-boosting task. Physical wellness may be another value, and going for regular walks outside could be a meaningful mood booster. List a few of your meaningful tasks below. If you need additional help, consider what your values are first (for example, learning, family, spirituality, or community) and then think about actions consistent with those values (for example, taking a woodworking course, having kids over for Sunday dinner, engaging in meditation practice, or attending a neighborhood park cleanup).

Meaningful tasks

- _____
- _____
- _____
- _____

We need a good balance of different mood-boosting activities in order to feel satisfied with our lives. If someone was engaged in only pleasurable tasks, for example, life might feel emptier in the absence of accomplishments or meaningful tasks. Keep in mind that behavioral activation should involve a combination of pleasure, mastery, and meaningful tasks.

STARTING BEHAVIORAL ACTIVATION

Let's look at a step-by-step guide to behavioral activation.

Behavioral Activation: Step 1

Identify a wide range of mood-boosting activities. You just got started with this step by identifying tasks that provide a sense of pleasure, mastery, and meaning. If you need additional inspiration for these tasks, you can consult the Mood-Boosting Activities List at http://www.new harbinger.com/51260. Alternatively, you could engage in some self-monitoring of your activities in a given week and try to notice whether any of the things you currently do provide a sense of pleasure, mastery, or meaning.

Behavioral Activation: Step 2

On a daily basis, pick at least one mood-boosting activity to engage in. The more mood-boosting activities you do, the better you will feel. Remember to start with something small and specific, especially if you are feeling depressed and your energy and motivation is at a premium. For instance, if you pick a mastery task of getting physical exercise, you may want to start with the smaller task "spend five minutes stretching." As we have mentioned, don't expect motivation to show up and grant you permission to engage in your mood-boosting activity. Focus on taking a small action and then evaluate how you feel *after.*

Behavioral Activation: Step 3

Rate your mood before and after the mood-boosting activity. When people are feeling depressed, they tend to feel pessimistic about the extent to which activities will feel good or boost their mood. In other words, they predict that nothing will help them feel better. This can often keep them stuck in the vicious cycle of activity disengagement that we reviewed earlier. Rating your mood before and after the task can help you gather more data to see whether the task made your mood better. Even if your mood stayed the same, the task can still be valuable in that it prevented your mood from getting worse. People may also have other reflections after engaging with behavioral activation that may help them on subsequent days. For example, if someone's mood is worse after going to a doctor's appointment, they may think ahead and for the next appointment, plan to meet a friend for lunch after to help them feel better.

Summary: Behavioral Activation Steps

To summarize, the three steps of behavioral activation are:

1. Identify a wide range of mood-boosting activities. Include tasks that provide a sense of pleasure, mastery, and meaning.
2. Pick at least one mood-boosting activity to engage in daily.
3. Rate your mood before and after the mood-boosting activity.

Below is a Behavioral Activation Tracking Form that captures these steps for conducting behavioral activation. We included a blank form in the "Putting CBT into Practice" section later in the chapter to help guide your behavioral activation. You can download additional copies of the form at http://www.newharbinger.com/512 60.

Here are Victor's responses as an example. For this worksheet the ratings for mood before and mood after are based on a scale of 1 to 10, with 10 being the most positive.

Behavioral Activation Tracking Form

Date	Mood-Boosting Activity *Note if pleasure, mastery, or meaning.*	Mood Before *Rate on a scale of 1 to 10.*	Mood After *Rate on a scale of 1 to 10.*	What Else Did I Learn or Experience?
Monday	Make appointment with financial advisor (meaning)	4	6	It feels good to be proactive about my finances.
Tuesday	Play guitar for fifteen minutes (pleasure and mastery)	2	4	I had some negative thoughts about my skill level, but I'm still glad I practiced.
Wednesday	Pick up prescription from pharmacy (mastery)	4	7	Pharmacist was very friendly and took his time with me.
Thursday	Go for thirty-minute walk (meaning)	3	3	I had back pain after. Maybe I should shorten the walk next time.
Friday	Play with grandkids in daughter's backyard (pleasure)	3	8	I had back pain and fatigue before. Seeing the kids laugh and play boosted my spirits.

Although the idea behind behavioral activation is a simple one, there's no denying that it becomes significantly more challenging when you're feeling depressed. It's helpful to return to the idea that motivation follows action—it doesn't just come before it. You will likely not feel like doing behavioral activation, so focus on the smallest possible action step you can take to break the cycle of disengagement and see what happens after. At the very least, you're practicing making choices and not letting depression do that for you.

Those are the basics of exposure therapy for anxiety and behavioral activation for depression. They are two powerful interventions that can help you limit the extent to which your fears and mood negatively impact your life. Collectively, they can help maximize your engagement in life and make your later years fulfilling and rewarding. Who wouldn't want that?

TAKE-HOME POINTS

- *Exposure therapy is an effective tool for reducing fear and anxiety across the lifespan.*
- *Exposure therapy involves repeatedly confronting situations, thoughts, physical sensations, or emotions that make you feel anxious in order to learn whether your fears are realistic and boost your confidence to deal with these situations.*
- *Behavioral activation is a powerful strategy for reducing depression and increasing engagement in your life.*
- *Behavioral activation involves picking mood-boosting activities to engage in daily and monitoring how this impacts your mood.*
- *Don't wait to feel motivated to engage in behavioral-activation activities. Motivation can come after taking action in a small way.*

PUTTING CBT INTO PRACTICE

Put your knowledge of exposure therapy and behavioral activation to good use and start engaging in one of the interventions this week. Follow the steps outlined in the chapter and track your progress using either the Exposure Therapy Tracking Form or the Behavioral Activation Tracking Form below. You can download additional copies of the forms from h ttp://www.newharbinger.com/51260. Keep in mind that change doesn't always happen quickly, especially if you've been feeling stuck in avoidance or withdrawal behaviors. You may need to stay engaged in doing exposure therapy and behavioral activation for a few weeks in order to get maximal benefit from them. If you notice your motivation waning, go back to chapter 4 on goal-setting. The decisional balance exercise you completed can be a helpful reminder of why you committed to doing CBT and things that can be challenging, such as exposure therapy and behavioral activation.

For this worksheet, rate your peak and end anxiety on a scale of 0 to 10, with 10 being the most intense and 0 being no anxiety.

Exposure Therapy Tracking Form

My Exposures	Date	Peak Anxiety *Rate on a scale of 0 to 10.*	End Anxiety *Rate on a scale of 0 to 10.*	What I Learned	Safety Behaviors I Avoided

Date	Mood-Boosting Activity (Note if pleasure, mastery, or meaning)	Mood Before *Rate on a scale of 1 to 10.*	Mood After *Rate on a scale of 1 to 10.*	What Else Did I Learn or Experience?

Behavioral Activation Tracking Form

WHAT'S NEXT?

- *Growing older can be full of ups and downs and present numerous challenges. Challenges can start to feel like daunting mountains to climb when you struggle with anxiety and depression.*

- *CBT offers a helpful framework for problem-solving that can allow people to adopt a more active role in dealing with challenges in life.*

CHAPTER 8

Problem-Solving

- *As you grow older, solving problems can become more challenging if you struggle with anxiety or depression.*
- *Viewing problems as threats, insisting on perfect solutions, and being under-resourced can make it more difficult to engage in effective problem-solving*
- *CBT offers a step-by-step approach to solving problems that involves defining the problem, brainstorming solutions, evaluating the solutions, implementing a solution, and evaluating the outcome.*

As much as growing older can bring a whole host of benefits, such as freedom from certain responsibilities (for example, childrearing or launching a career), more time to explore hobbies and interests, and wisdom and emotional maturity, many new challenges can emerge.

Medical issues need attention and depending on their severity, may require ongoing care and decision-making about how to best manage them. Certain tasks that were easy in the past, such as housework, may be harder to do now and may require additional help from others. You may need to change how you accomplish everyday tasks, such as finding alternative transportation if you don't drive anymore. You could be considering a change in your living situation or wondering whether you can manage independently anymore. Financial pressures can also mount in late life for a variety of reasons, such as having a reduced income in retirement, additional health care expenses, or supporting significant others or family members. Stressors can also emerge from being a caregiver (for example, for a spouse, adult child, or grandchild).

There's no shortage of problems in late life, and if you're feeling overwhelmed by the ones on your plate, you're not alone. Take a few moments to reflect on and write down the problems (however big or small) in your life currently.

Problem list

- _____
- _____
- _____
- _____

How does it feel to see your problems written down? Do you notice any feelings of being overwhelmed, confused, indecisive, or all of the above? If so, you're in good company. We're happy to reassure you that part of your CBT tool kit for growing older also includes help with solving these problems. It may seem like problem-solving should be intuitive, but this isn't always the case.

CBT provides a structured approach to problem-solving where you work through a series of steps to guide you toward an actionable solution. This is tremendously helpful for the problems in our lives where there is in fact something you can do about it. The best way to deal with those types of issues is to take action, and in doing so, you will likely find an improvement in your mood.

The first part of this chapter will speak to why problem-solving can be a challenge for anyone, and particularly when you're anxious or depressed. Then, we'll outline a step-by-step approach to problem-solving. We'll provide a number of examples from the characters you've met in the book so far. We'll also tie together some of the strategies you've learned with problem-solving, for example, changing thoughts, and exposures. Let's get going.

WHY IS PROBLEM-SOLVING CHALLENGING?

Problem-solving may seem like something we do automatically, and to a certain extent that's true. If you've made it this far in life, you've likely done very well at solving a wide variety of problems. However, growing older can mean you face different types of problems that may become more challenging to deal with. Why is that?

Seeing Problems as Threats

One barrier to solving problems can stem from how we view the problems themselves. It's not uncommon for people, especially those who struggle with anxiety and depression, to see problems as threats. They may seem like insurmountable mountains that they just can't possibly climb. People may lack confidence in their abilities to make a choice and cope with the consequences. They may fear making the wrong choice and making a situation worse. Have you ever experienced something like this? You wouldn't be the only one. It's not uncommon when you're feeling overwhelmed or vulnerable to respond to problems as if they are threats.

But viewing problems in this way creates more anxiety or hopelessness and can make you want to avoid a problem altogether. As an alternative, you can recast problems as challenges that provide opportunities for growth. Life's challenges can offer us a chance to use our strengths (or cultivate new ones), generate creative solutions, work cooperatively with others and potentially deepen relationships, and boost our self-confidence. If you're having a difficult time thinking about problems in this way, think about a challenge in your life that you've overcome. Perhaps you struggled academically in school, immigrated to a new country, or started a new career at some point during your working years. How did you cope with this challenge? How might it have changed you for the better? Is it possible that your current problems have the same potential for growth?

Rejecting Imperfect Solutions

Another common barrier to solving problems has to do with how we view solutions. Individuals who are perfectionistic, meaning they have unrealistic or unrelenting standards, may be inclined to seek perfect solutions. While this may sound appealing and aspirational, the reality of our messy and imperfect world is that there are rarely perfect solutions. While that may feel discouraging, let's not forget that imperfect solutions can still get a job done. Helmets, seatbelts, and parachutes are all less than a hundred percent effective, and yet people use them despite that. Imperfect solutions can still be effective and are usually better than no solutions at all. Especially if you want to skydive more than once.

Having Limited Resources

Solving life's problems is a lot easier when you've got more resources at your disposal, whether that be time, family, friends, money, stable housing, access to health care, physical mobility, or cognitive functioning, among many other things. Conversely, it can feel daunting and discouraging to attempt to face life's challenges when you feel lacking in different types of resources or supports. It can also be challenging to increase access to resources (for example, social support) when you need them the most. Because few people will be abundantly resourced across all domains of their life (and if you are, lucky you!), we are inevitably required to try to solve life's problems with the resources we have at our disposal. It doesn't mean we won't be able to handle challenges, but it does mean assessing what your resources are and making the most of what you have. You may find there may be upsides to using the resources you have even if the situation is not ideal. An older adult without a spouse may lean more into friendships to help meet their needs and solve problems, for example. Nothing helps deepen friendships more than going through hardships together.

With these challenges in mind, let's review a process for problem-solving you can work through help you meet these issues head-on and take steps to improve your life where possible.

STEP-BY-STEP PROBLEM-SOLVING

To help understand how to engage in problem-solving more effectively, let's look at different examples of challenges faced by Tina and Victor.

Tina's problems

Tina has been feeling more anxious lately about how to manage caregiving demands for her husband. He was diagnosed with multiple sclerosis five years ago and has experienced a worsening of his symptoms. His mobility, vision, and bowel function are increasingly affected. He is needing more and more help with activities of daily living, such as dressing himself, moving around the house, toileting, and meal preparation. Tina has been trying the best she can to care for him herself but is finding this very difficult emotionally and physically. It often means she can't leave her husband or go out for longer periods of time. She feels more isolated socially and physically worn out.

Victor's problems

Victor has been experiencing more conflict in his relationship with his daughter and son-in-law. His daughter often seems irritated with him, and his son-in-law seems to be more distant. Victor's daughter has made comments alluding to his lack of support and presence in her family's life, for example, "You missed your grandson's soccer practice again" and "I thought you'd be around to help more when you moved closer to us." Victor's daughter and son-in-law also made a request for his financial help to help them purchase a larger home, to which he hasn't committed to. Victor feels guilty knowing that his daughter doesn't think he is available and supportive but also feels resentful about her expectations of him, which he feels are unrealistic at times.

Now it's your turn. Elaborate on the problems you identified earlier in this chapter.

Let's use the examples from Tina and Victor to go through a step-by-step process for problem-solving.

Step 1: Identify the Problem

Yes, we know this is an obvious first step that you didn't need two psychologists to point out. But oftentimes, we can get stuck solving a problem because we haven't accurately or specifically defined what it is, who it involves, and when the problem is occurring. For example, if we defined Tina's main problem as her husband's health issue that doesn't necessarily tell us what specifically the concern is or enable us to find helpful solutions. As you identify problems, make sure you identify *who* is involved, *what* the specific problem is and if applicable, *when* the problem is occurring. This can set you up to generate solutions and implement them more effectively. A more specific set of problems are identified for Tina and Victor below.

	Problem Identification
Tina	I can't consistently dress, bathe, and prepare meals for my husband every day
	I can't leave the house for more than four hours at time.
Victor	Daughter expects me to see her family whenever possible.
	Daughter wants my financial support this month for a down payment.

Now it's your turn. Try to identify your problem more specifically, making sure to highlight *who* and *what* is involved and *when* the problem is occurring.

Problem Identification

Step 2: Brainstorm Possible Solutions

In the brainstorming phase of problem-solving, the goal is to consider as many possible solutions to your problem as you can. It's not to evaluate the solutions just yet but to consider as many ways out of the problem as you can think of. Even if they're a little silly. Even if they're a lot silly! Can't find anyone to go on vacation with? Ever consider going to the beach with a blow-up doll fashioned after your best friend? Some research demonstrates that humor and positive moods help us generate novel solutions to problems that we may not have considered otherwise (Shen et al. 2019). Have some fun with brainstorming solutions whenever it's possible. At the very least, consider any and all solutions even if they seem unfeasible or impractical on the surface. Let's see where Tina and Victor went with this step below.

	Problem Identification	Brainstorming Solutions
Tina	I can't consistently dress, bathe, and prepare meals for my husband every day. I can't leave the house for more than four hours at time.	Hire a part-time nursing aide to help with care Ask friends and neighbors to assist with meal preparation and dressing Move husband to an assisted-living facility Hire full-time chef to do meal preparation Move in with adult children to get their support
Victor	Daughter expects me to see her family whenever possible. Daughter wants my financial support this month for a down payment.	Be over at daughter's house every day Have conversation about realistic expectations Hire stunt double when I'm not available to go to grandson's soccer games Give daughter money for down payment Give money for down payment with repayment plan Decline request for money for a down payment and offer financial support in another manner (for example, educational savings accounts for grandkids)

Now it's your chance to get brainstorming any and all possible solutions to the problems you identified in step 1.

Problem Identification	Brainstorming Solutions

Step 3: Evaluate Solutions

After thoroughly engaging in brainstorming, now's the time to evaluate each solution. Go through each and identify the pros and cons. What are the upsides and downsides? In this process, you might eliminate some solutions (especially the comedic ones) rather quickly if you know they will be impractical or not feasible. You can cross those solutions out. In evaluating your solutions, also keep in mind both the short- and long-term benefits or costs of each. Sometimes what can seem like an unfavorable solution now might actually be for the best in the long term. The alternative can also be true, with what seems like a good short-term solution not being sustainable over the long term. Remember what we said earlier in the chapter: there are no perfect solutions. You are looking for the solution with the best balance of pros to cons. An imperfect solution can still be good enough to deal with the problem at hand. Let's see how Tina and Victor evaluated their solutions.

Tina's Solution Evaluation

Problem: I can't consistently dress, bathe, and prepare meals for my husband every day. I can't leave the house for more than four hours at time.

	Brainstorming Solutions	Evaluate Solutions
Option A	Hire a part-time nursing aide to help with care	Pro: Allows me to better take care of myself Pro: Husband might get better care Con: Additional cost each month
Option B	Ask friends and neighbors to assist with meal preparation and dressing	Pro: Save cost of hiring someone Con: Friends and neighbors may not always be available or capable of helping over the long term
Option C	Move husband to an assisted-living facility	Pro: Help is available around the clock Pro: He will need more help over the long term Con: Husband not ready for this move yet Con: I'd be lonely
Option D	Hire full-time chef to do meal preparation	
Option E	Move in with adult children to get their support	

Victor's Solution Evaluation

Problem: Daughter expects me to see her family whenever possible. Daughter wants my financial support this month for a down payment.

	Brainstorming Solutions	Evaluate Solutions
Option A	Be over at daughter's house every day	Pro: Daughter is satisfied Con: I get fatigued and resentful Con: We get on one another's nerves over time
Option B	Have conversation about realistic expectations	Pro: Daughter knows how much she can realistically expect me to be over Pro: I have the time I need to take care of myself and the house Pro: We enjoy the time we spend together more Con: She may be upset with me for not being over every day but that could be short term
Option C	~~Hire stunt double when I'm not available to go to grandson's soccer games~~	
Option D	~~Give daughter money for down payment~~	
Option E	Give money for down payment with repayment plan	Pro: Daughter will be pleased Pro: I'll get the money back eventually Con: It may put some financial pressure on me now
Option F	Decline request for money for a down payment and offer financial support in another manner (for example, educational savings accounts for grandkids)	Pro: Still supporting daughter and grandkids but in a more financially sustainable way Con: Daughter may be unhappy with me

You guessed it, now it's your turn to evaluate your solutions. Consider the pros and cons of each as well as which might be better short-term or long-term solutions.

Your Solution Evaluation

Problem Identification: _____

_____

	Brainstorming Solutions	Evaluate Solutions
Option A		
Option B		
Option C		
Option D		
Option E		

Step 4: Commit to a Solution and Evaluate Outcome

The last step in the problem-solving process involves taking action—implementing one of the solutions you identified and then reflecting on the outcome. How did the solution work?

Depending on how things go, you may need to go back to other solutions if one doesn't pan out as expected or your circumstances change. For example, Tina may decide to pay for part-time help to assist her husband with dressing and bathing only to find out that her husband's needs are increasing and warrant a move to an assisted-living facility. When faced with complex situations that can evolve and change, we often need to shift solutions with time but always keep focused on doing what works to help us meet our goals.

Here are the outcomes and evaluations for the examples from Tina and Victor. You can download blank copies of the Problem-Solving Worksheet at http://www.newharbinger.com/512 60.

Tina's Problem-Solving Worksheet

Tina's Problem: I can't consistently dress, bathe, and prepare meals for my husband every day. I can't leave the house for more than four hours at time.

	Brainstorming Solutions	Evaluate Solutions	Commit to Solution and Evaluate Outcome
Option A	Hire a part-time nursing aide to help with care	Pro: Allows me to better take care of myself Pro: Husband might get better care Con: Additional cost each month	Outcome: Had to wait to find someone suitable, but once help was secured, I felt relieved. It seems worth the cost, all things considered.
Option B	Ask friends and neighbors to assist with meal preparation and dressing	Pro: Save cost of hiring someone Con: Friends and neighbors may not always be available or capable of helping over the long term	
Option C	Move husband to an assisted-living facility	Pro: Help is available around the clock Pro: He will need more help over the long term Con: Husband not ready for this move yet Con: I'd be lonely	

Victor's Problem-Solving Worksheet

Victor's Problem: Daughter expects me to see her family whenever possible. Daughter wants my financial support this month for a down payment.

	Brainstorming Solutions	Evaluate Solutions	Commit to Solution and Evaluate Outcome
Option A	Be over at daughter's house every day	Pro: Daughter is satisfied Con: I get fatigued and resentful Con: We get on one another's nerves over time	
Option B	Have conversation about realistic expectations	Pro: Daughter knows how much she can realistically expect me to be over Pro: I have the time I need to take care of myself and the house Pro: We enjoy the time we spend together more Con: She may be upset with me for not being over every day but that could be short-term	Outcome: Daughter was disappointed but also more understanding than I expected. The grandkids get more excited when I come over now.
Option C	Give money for down payment with repayment plan	Pro: Daughter will be pleased Pro: I'll get the money back eventually Con: It may put some financial pressure on me now	Outcome: Daughter and son-in-law were appreciative of the help and open to a repayment plan.
Option D	Decline request for money for a down payment and offer financial support in another manner (for example, educational savings accounts for grandkids)	Pro: Still supporting daughter and grandkids but in a more financially sustainable way Con: Daughter may be unhappy with me	

You're up. It's your time to select a solution to implement to help solve your problem. After you do so, evaluate the outcome. Use the

Problem-Solving Worksheet in the "Putting CBT into Practice" section later in this chapter or download the worksheet from http://www.newh arbinger.com/51260.

Problem-Solving Worksheet

Problem Identification: _____

	Brainstorming Solutions	Evaluate Solutions	Commit to Solution and Evaluate Outcome
Option A			
Option B			
Option C			
Option D			
Option E			

You've now got a solid understanding of how a CBT approach to problem-solving can assist you in navigating some of the challenges that emerge in late life. It's not to say this is easy, however. There are plenty of things that can get in the way of approaching and solving problems when you struggle with anxiety or depression. Earlier in the chapter, we highlighted how seeing problems as threats, insisting on perfect solutions, and being under-resourced can make it difficult to navigate challenges that come up as you age. Aside from using the problem-solving framework here, are there any other strategies you've learned so far in the book that could come in handy when attempting to solve problems? We can think of a few. Let's review how some of the strategies covered in the book thus far can come in handy when it comes to tackling problems.

SELF-MONITORING

In chapter 5, you engaged in self-monitoring of your emotions, thoughts, behaviors, and physical sensations—a useful tool to assist in changing your reactions to any of these experiences. This can also be a valuable tool to enlist in your efforts to problem-solve. By reviewing your self-monitoring logs, you can help identify problems that need solving. For example, let's say you recorded that you were feeling sad and lonely on a Friday evening and your thoughts were *I wish I had more to do in the evenings* and *Everyone else seems busy with other things*. This can help you identify that you want to find other ways to spend your time in the evening and socialize more. You might consider joining a social club, reach out to friends to arrange a future get-together, attend an exercise class on a Friday evening, or attempt to make small talk with people at the park or at church. Your self-monitoring logs can be a good tool to help assist with identifying problems amenable to solving.

CHANGING THOUGHTS

You learned in chapter 6 about how our thoughts can become extreme or unhelpful when dealing with anxiety or depression and how attempting to change our thinking can impact how we feel and behave. You can put this knowledge to good use by examining your thinking patterns while you're problem-solving. Keep an eye out for the cognitive distortions we discussed in chapter 5, such as black-and-white thinking, catastrophizing, and mental filtering.

Let's take a look at Tina's thoughts about finding help for her husband, for example. In considering paying for part-time help for her husband, she has the thought *That will put me into financial ruin.* Does that sound like a cognitive distortion, and if so, which one? Assuming Tina is in a reasonably good financial situation, it could be catastrophizing. When she has that thought, she could use any one of the questions highlighted in chapter 6 to help examine the thought a little more closely. She could engage in evidence-gathering and explore the degree to which getting paid help will actually be a financial strain and how much she could afford. After doing so, she might conclude that yes, paid help is an additional expense but one that she can offset by cutting other expenses. She may also conclude that spending the money could be worth it if her husband has better care and she takes better care of herself physically and emotionally. Practicing examining and changing her thinking could help Tina be more open to implementing solutions and feel more satisfied with them.

As another example let's take a look at Victor. When he considers having a conversation with his daughter to tell her that he can't realistically be over at her house every day, he may think, *Unless I'm over there every day, we won't have a good relationship.* Does that sound like a cognitive distortion, and if so, which one? It could be all-or-nothing thinking. Victor could use any number of questions to help examine this thought further. One helpful question could be: what's another interpretation of this situation? Victor may acknowledge that even if he's not at his daughter's place every day, they can still have a good relationship. It may be even better if he's not there every day so he has more opportunities to take care of himself, leading to better quality of time spent with his daughter. Like with Tina, we can see how examining and changing thinking could lead Victor to feel better about a proposed solution and be more willing to implement it. We would encourage you to examine your thinking as you engage in problem-solving.

EXPOSURE THERAPY AND BEHAVIORAL ACTIVATION

Chapter 7 provided an overview of exposure therapy and behavioral activation—two behavioral interventions to help reduce anxiety and depression, respectively. Any ideas as to how these might relate to problem-solving?

The process of engaging in exposure therapy or behavioral activation might require some problem-solving. For example, someone facing a fear of driving may need to engage in problem-solving to figure out how they might find upcoming opportunities to face their fears (for example, offer to drive a spouse to the airport, drive to a dental appointment instead of taking public transit, or drive to the library during rush hour instead of off-hours). Alternatively, someone engaging in behavioral activation might want to get more physical exercise but be limited in the types of activity they can engage in due to an injury or disability. They might engage in problem-solving to help identify possible solutions to this (for example, work with a personal trainer or physiotherapist, look up exercises that can be done with the upper body only, walk shorter distances, or stick to swimming).

From another perspective, implementing one of the solutions you identified may be a form of exposure or behavioral activation. For example, if Victor commits to going to his grandson's soccer games, this could be a form of behavioral activation for him. It could be a meaningful task because it is connected to one of his values, family. Likewise, if Tina opts to ask for help from neighbors and friends to assist with her husband's care, this could be a form of exposure if asking for help is something that makes her feel anxious. So, problem-solving can end up being part of your efforts to face your fears or boost your mood. Another reason to get engaged with it.

NEED MORE HELP?

If you're encountering issues with any of the problem-solving steps we've outlined, you may want to enlist the help of a trusted friend, family member, or health care professional. You could ask others for their assistance in brainstorming or evaluating solutions, for example. We usually don't solve our problems in isolation and taking advantage of the help and insights offered by others can go a long way in helping us deal with the challenges of aging. List the persons below whom you might be able to approach for help with problem-solving if you need it.

TAKE-HOME POINTS

• *Problem-solving can be more difficult when you feel depressed or anxious.*

• *It can be helpful to view problems as challenges and opportunities for growth.*

• *Your willingness to accept imperfect solutions and use whatever resources you have at your disposal is key to dealing with challenges in your life.*

• *Problem-solving in CBT involves defining the problem, brainstorming solutions, evaluating and implementing solutions, and assessing the outcome.*

• *Other CBT strategies can be useful to incorporate into problem -solving, for example, self-monitoring, changing your thinking, exposure therapy, and behavioral activation.*

PUTTING CBT INTO PRACTICE

Practice engaging in problem-solving this week. Review one of the other problems you listed earlier in this chapter and use the step-by-step process to help you solve the problem. You can download additional copies of the Problem-Solving Worksheet at http://www.n ewharbinger.com/51260. Remember to consider using other CBT strategies you've learned thus far to help you solve problems, for example, self-monitoring, changing your thinking, exposure therapy, and behavioral activation. Other people can be great resource to consult if you need additional help with this process.

Problem-Solving Worksheet

Problem Identification: _____

_____

	Brainstorming Solutions	Evaluate Solutions	Commit to Solution and Evaluate Outcome
Option A			
Option B			
Option C			
Option D			
Option E			

WHAT'S NEXT?

- *There are many things about growing older that we can't change or problem-solve our way out of.*
- *Acceptance is a misunderstood concept that is difficult to cultivate for many.*
- *We will help define what acceptance means (and doesn't mean) and how to practice this in your own life.*

CHAPTER 9

Accepting What You Can't Control (And Focusing on What You Can)

- *There are many things about growing older that we can't change. While acceptance is often needed in these situations, it can be difficult to achieve.*
- *Acceptance is an acknowledgement of the present moment as it is, not the way you'd like it to be, as well as a willingness to work with it as opposed to against it.*
- *Acceptance does not mean approval or resignation.*
- *We can practice acceptance using a number of strategies, such as mental imagery, RAIN, and mindfulness meditation.*

One of the most challenging aspects of growing older (or maybe being a human in general) is being faced with difficult circumstances that are outside of your control. Let's face it, there is an awful lot that we can't change about our lives and the people in it. The previous chapter focused on engaging in problem-solving for issues in your life where there may be solutions. But what do we do when we face challenges that we can't change or alter in a meaningful way? You guessed it, that's where acceptance comes in. This chapter will focus, first, on defining acceptance, a concept that is frequently misunderstood. We'll speak to why it's important to cultivate acceptance and highlight areas of life where it might be needed. The latter portion of the chapter will focus on strategies to help encourage acceptance in your own life, and as you'll see, it can be a powerful force for change and emotional well-being.

WHAT IS ACCEPTANCE? (AND WHAT IT ISN'T)

To help understand what acceptance is and what it isn't, consider the last time you were stuck in traffic. What were you thinking at the time? If you're like many people, you could have had any number of different thoughts: *Why did I take this route? What's the big hold up? When will traffic start to move? If only people were more sensible drivers. This screws up my entire day!* You likely felt annoyed, impatient, and agitated. Although this is a very human reaction (most of us would have these thoughts and feelings), it's very different from acceptance.

To understand what acceptance is, it can be helpful at first to clarify what it *isn't*. There are a number of misconceptions about and misunderstandings of this concept that make it difficult for us to cultivate. Let's explore three misconceptions about acceptance a little further.

Misconception: Acceptance Means Approval

One of the first misunderstandings of acceptance is that it requires us to approve of or agree with something. Thankfully, that just isn't so. Accepting a situation, person, or ourselves doesn't require you to like, condone, or be okay with what is happening. If you've been diagnosed with a major medical condition, you don't need to like it in order to accept it—just like you don't have to agree with your daughter's way of parenting to come to terms with it. This idea may come as a relief if you've thought approval was a part of acceptance. Thankfully, acceptance has very little to do with how we evaluate a situation and more about our attitude toward and reaction to a situation.

Misconception: Acceptance Means Surrendering

A second common misconception of acceptance is that it means you've resigned yourself to a situation. You've given up. For example, in response to hearing that your sibling has accepted a terminal cancer diagnosis, you might feel angry and prematurely conclude that they're "giving up the good fight." While it's fair to say that having a serious illness requires a person to relinquish control in many aspects of life, it's short-sighted to call this, alone, acceptance. Acceptance involves equal acknowledgement of what is both within and not within your control. It's not about giving up. In acknowledging what we do and do not have control over, we are better able to focus on the things we can change and make better now. Your sibling can embody acceptance by acknowledging their lifespan is limited while also taking action to better their final few months, for example, getting information about pain-management options, creating an end-of-life plan, and remaining connected to valued relationships and activities as much as possible. From this perspective, acceptance means exercising your power to create desired change where it is possible and recognizing what can't be changed.

Misconception: Acceptance Is Easy

How often have you been told by other people during a challenging situation to let it go? It is something commonly encouraged and implies that acceptance should somehow be easily done to put difficult emotions behind us. Wouldn't that be nice? The reality is that acceptance can be exceptionally difficult. Accepting ourselves, for example, is often a lifelong journey that is rarely linear or simple. You may have thought that you accepted your body only to find later in life that as it creates more problems and doesn't cooperate reliably, you feel dissatisfied with it. Acceptance can be challenging, but acknowledging that it is an ongoing and nonlinear process that takes intentional practice can help reduce unrealistic expectations that it should be easy.

DEFINING ACCEPTANCE

With the misconceptions in mind, where does that leave us with what acceptance is? The psychologist Marsha Linehan wrote about the idea of *radical acceptance,* which she defined as being a complete, wholehearted acknowledgement of the present moment as it is, without judgement (2015). The phrase "It is what it is" helps encapsulate this. You can also think of acceptance as a willingness to greet what life offers you. The Latin roots of the word acceptance mean to take or receive what is offered. If we adopt a more accepting stance within our lives and in doing so, willingly acknowledge what life offers us moment to moment without judgement, we can often find our experience transformed. Acceptance can help us stop fighting what is and use our energy to figure out how to respond.

Let's take the example presented earlier of being stuck in traffic. Accepting this situation might start with acknowledging that you feel angry about being stuck and not judging yourself for feeling this way (it's neither bad nor good to feel angry, it just is). It may also involve recognizing that you don't have control over how fast the traffic is going, but you can focus on bettering the moment by taking a few deep breaths, putting some music on, and singing along as loud as you can.

As another example, accepting physical changes that come with aging might start with recognizing that you feel sad and frustrated that you aren't as youthful as you used to be and not judging yourself for feeling this way (it's a very human reaction, after all). It may also involve acknowledging that you won't be able to do certain things that you used to, such as going for a strenuous hike, and extending some understanding and grace to yourself by taking breaks and giving yourself pep talks (*I'm doing the best I can*). You might even use the slower pace as a chance to take in more of what's going on around you.

Acceptance might look and sound different depending on the person and circumstance, but ultimately, it has us turning toward our emotional reactions to life's challenges and asking ourselves, *How can I work with this?*

WHAT NEEDS ACCEPTING?

There are many aspects of our lives that require some degree of acceptance. These include external circumstances and forces that you can't control, such as other people's behavior, the actions of systems and institutions, and global issues, such as the COVID-19 pandemic or climate change. There are a whole host of individual experiences that warrant acceptance, such as awareness of your mortality, changes to and challenges with your body, your upbringing and family history, and personal strengths and weaknesses. From the characters introduced in the book, let's look at several areas in life they identified as not being within their control and needing acceptance.

Example	Situations to Accept
Tina (generalized anxiety)	My husband's illness is progressive. The financial markets will fluctuate. I don't have complete control over my grandkids' well-being.
Fred (social anxiety)	I won't really know or be able to control what people think of me. I can't control all physical symptoms of anxiety.
Alice (health anxiety)	I lack of total control of my body. I can't control all the choices made by medical professionals.

Example	Situations to Accept
Jim (panic disorder)	I will feel anxious. My fight-flight-freeze response is normal and not up to me to stop.
Victor (major depressive disorder)	I can't control my daughter's expectations of me. I made mistakes in my career that I can't take back.

Many of the thoughts and feelings we experience daily warrant acceptance as well because you don't choose the types of thoughts that pop into your head or the immediate emotional reactions you have. Remember that just because we accept our thoughts and feelings doesn't mean that there's nothing you can do about them. As we've mentioned, acceptance does not mean resignation—quite the opposite. Usually as we accept what can't be changed (including some of our thoughts and feelings), we are more able to focus on the aspects that can. As psychologist Carl Rogers said, "Once I accept myself as I am, then I can change" (1995).

From what we've described above, can you identify aspects of your life that are in part (or entirely) out of your control where you could benefit from acceptance? Write some of them down here.

_____

_____

_____

_____

_____

_____

WHY ACCEPT?

Marsha Linehan, who coined the term radical acceptance, wisely points out why acceptance is so important. She highlights that while we will all experience pain in our life (for example, loss, heartbreak, regret, guilt, and longing), pain turns into suffering when we cannot accept it (Linehan 2015). It is often our initial impulse to deny, avoid, or suppress pain (the opposite of acceptance). Refusal to accept our physical limitations, for example, may mean that we do things to exacerbate them, such as carry on with activities that worsen physical pain. In whatever form pain comes, whether it's emotional or physical, it is made worse when we don't accept it. Although acceptance of it doesn't necessarily reduce the pain we feel in our lives (this part is unavoidable), it does reduce our suffering. Ultimately, acceptance allows us to more fully participate in our own lives.

HOW TO PRACTICE ACCEPTANCE

How exactly do we cultivate more acceptance in our lives? This might be especially important as we age and as growing older presents new challenges that may be difficult to come to terms with. The remainder of this chapter outlines three different ways in which we can cultivate more acceptance: using mental imagery, practicing RAIN (recognize, allow, investigate, nurture), and engaging in mindfulness meditation. We'll describe each in more detail and encourage you to practice each in a small way after each section.

Mental Imagery

The use of mental imagery can be a powerful way to illustrate abstract concepts like acceptance in a way that we're likely to understand and use in a more concrete way. Let's explore a metaphor that can help you create mental images to assist you in having a greater level of acceptance for your thoughts and feelings.

Imagine you're hosting a party. Acceptance sounds fun already, doesn't it? Instead of being an invite-only shindig, this is more of an open house. You're not entirely sure who is going to show up and when, or how long your guests will stay. One of the first guests to arrive, and early at that, is anxiety. What do you imagine anxiety talks about at the party? It'll vary from person to person, but it will usually start talking about the variety of different things that could go wrong at the party: *We won't have enough seating* or *What's that smell? The kitchen must be on fire!* This well-intentioned guest is preoccupied with possible mishaps and dangers.

Then, in walks another guest, depression (slowly, and dragging its feet). It has a different agenda at the party: focus on all the negatives and cast a shadow on just about anything it can. *This isn't going to be much fun. I don't know why I even bother coming to parties. People don't find me interesting anyway.* Many other guests pop and in and out, such as guilt, regret, shame, and anger—each with its own message and motivation. None of them are ill-intentioned, and each serves a purpose in its own way (as we discussed about emotions in chapter 5).

Take a moment to reflect on what emotional guests would be at your party and list them here.

Your job as the party host is to decide how exactly you want to respond to your guests, even the uninvited ones. You might try at first to ignore them entirely. While you might be successful in pretending that you're alone at the party, those party guests usually have a way of making themselves known and drawing your attention even more. You might try then try getting angry with the guests *(Who invited you?)* and attempt to kick them out. But it doesn't feel great to try to kick all those guests out, and there's no guarantee that you'd be successful.

Where does that leave you, our lovely host? Let's consider what would be in the best interest of both you and your guests. First, it can be helpful to acknowledge who's arrived even if they're unexpected or undesired, for example, *Hello, anxiety* or *Welcome, depression.* Next, consider speaking to them with as much patience, understanding, and wisdom as you can summon. After all, isn't that how you'd like to be treated? For example, *I appreciate your concern, anxiety. I know you mean well and are just looking out for me. From what I can tell, we are safe right now. Let's chat later in the party.* How about for depression? *I know you're feeling down, and I understand how hard it is to feel that way. Sometimes things can play out better than you expect. Let's focus on what we can do to feel a little better in this moment.*

We can't control who shows up at the party, how long they stay, or what they talk about. But as the host, you can decide how to respond to guests that show up. Acknowledging, understanding, and providing words of wisdom to those party guests is ultimately a way to extend acceptance, kindness, and love to yourself.

How might you respond to the emotional guests you listed above? Try to formulate a response that acknowledges the emotion and extends understanding, patience, and wisdom. Write it down.

Let It RAIN

The psychologist Tara Brach developed the acronym RAIN (recognize, allow, investigate, nurture) to help guide efforts to accept and be more compassionate with ourselves when we experience emotional pain (2020). This can be a useful framework to use to process our feelings when they feel overwhelming and direct kindness and compassion inward. Once you are more familiar with the steps of RAIN, you may want to close your eyes and walk through the process.

RECOGNIZE

First, take some time to notice and name any feelings you may be experiencing, such as sadness, anger, guilt, anxiety, or frustration. You may also want to identify areas in your body where you notice your emotions, such as tension in your shoulders, a heaviness in your chest, or knot in your stomach.

ALLOW

As much as you can, give your emotions space to be present just as they are. Don't try to stop them, control them, suppress them, or avoid feeling them. Allow your experience to be as it is.

INVESTIGATE

With an attitude of gentle curiosity, take interest in your experience by asking, *Where might I be feeling this emotion?* Ask yourself what part of you needs attention or what you might be needing, given what you are feeling.

NURTURE

With whatever you are observing, and particularly if it feels painful, try to greet your experience with some form of self-compassion. There are many ways we can be self-compassionate and what we need might vary depending on what we are feeling. For example, if you feel guilty you may need forgiveness. If you feel down and hopeless, you may need encouragement. If you're scared, you may need reassurance. Self-compassion may sound different depending on the person, but examples of it could be: *It's ok to be imperfect. I forgive you. I'm here with you. It's not your fault.* You might also consider a self-compassionate gesture, such as putting a hand over your heart.

After trying the process of RAIN, reflect on your experience. What do you notice in your body? How do you feel emotionally? Gently congratulate yourself for being in the presence of your own emotions and seeking to understand them and take care of yourself. Record some of your observations.

Mindfulness Meditation

You may or may not be familiar with some forms of meditation, but they have very much worked their way in the mainstream in the past twenty years in particular. A form of meditation called *mindfulness* is a particularly helpful way to cultivate more awareness of and acceptance for your present moment experience.

Jon Kabat-Zinn was one of the pioneers of the modern mindfulness meditation movement. He defined mindfulness in one of his seminal books *Wherever You Go, There You Ar* e as a way of "paying attention in a particular way: on purpose, in the present moment, and nonjudgmentally" (2009). This contrasts with how we usually pay attention, which can be scattered, dodging back and forth between the future, present, and past, and always evaluating or judging our experiences (for example, this is better/worse, bad/good, or too much/not enough). The latter is referred to as *doing mode*. With mindfulness meditation, we practice *being mode*, wherein we're not concerned about evaluating our experience or getting to a particular endpoint. Instead, we're focused on exploring and being curious about our present experience, just as it is.

In 1979, Kabat-Zinn initially developed a program of mindfulness meditation for his patients at a stress-reduction clinic at the University of Massachusetts. His patients were primarily individuals suffering with a wide range of chronic physical illnesses. In learning the philosophy and practice of mindfulness meditation, the patients found that they were better able to cope with their physical ailments, and their symptoms of anxiety reduced significantly (1982). Since then, there has been an exponential increase in the amount of research exploring the applications of mindfulness meditation to treating a wide variety of conditions, such as depression, stress, substance abuse, and illness. A variety of research supports the idea that mindfulness meditation can be a powerful practice that helps cultivate inner peace and acceptance.

How do you exactly engage in mindfulness meditation? How do you pay attention to the present moment without judgment? A good place to start is by using guided a mindfulness meditation practice. We provide instructions below for practicing mindfulness using an object.

MINDFULNESS MEDITATION WITH AN OBJECT

It can be helpful as you begin to practice mindfulness to use an object at first, as opposed to focusing on your thoughts and feelings. To start, pick one household object that's nearby, such as a pen or a mug. Next, practice examining this object as if it were the first time you've seen it in your life. Notice its shape, color, texture, and temperature. Describe it to yourself and as best you can, avoid evaluating it or judging it (for example, as bad, good, or ugly). As you do this, you will notice your mind drift to other thoughts, such as whether you're doing the exercise right, what you're going to do after the exercise, where you purchased the object, or what you ate for breakfast. When you catch this happening, congratulate yourself for noticing and then gently escort your attention back to the object. You will do this, inevitably, over and over. That is just what minds do. After several minutes exploring the object, you can end the mindfulness practice. Take a few moments to write out what you observed (for example, *My mind went to the future* or *I noticed feelings of boredom*). It's important to know that there are no wrong observations or experiences during a mindfulness practice. Simply let your experience be what it is.

You can practice mindfulness meditation in a number of different ways. You practiced here with an object, but you can extend that practice to everyday tasks, such as washing dishes, showering, brushing your teeth, or walking. You can also consult online resources or apps for guided mindfulness meditations that you can listen to. They vary in length (for example, five minutes to thirty minutes) and in focus (for example, mindful breathing, body scan, or loving-kindness meditation). Here are resources you can consult for guided mindfulness meditations and general information on mindfulness:

Websites
- Mindful (http://www.mindful.org)
- Headspace (http://www.headspace.com)

Books
- *Full Catastrophe Living* by Jon Kabat-Zinn (2013)
- *Wherever You Go, There You Are* by Jon Kabat-Zinn (2005)
- *The Mindful Way Through Anxiety* by Susan Orsillo and Lizabeth Roemer (2011)

- *The Mindful Way Through Depression* by Mark Williams, John Teasdale, Zindel Segal, and Jon Kabat-Zinn (2007)

As you start to incorporate a regular mindfulness meditation practice into your life, a number of common questions may emerge. Let's review a few so you are more aware.

SHOULD MINDFULNESS HELP ME CLEAR MY HEAD?

Many people assume that during a mindfulness meditation practice, they should be able to rid themselves of all their thoughts or at the very least the negative ones. These people will find themselves quickly disappointed and frustrated when they realize that it is impossible to get rid of our thoughts entirely. Mindfulness meditation doesn't help us clear our heads, but it does help us observe our thoughts and learn how to be flexible about where we're focusing our attention. It helps us relate to our thoughts as if they were items going down a conveyor belt. We can't stop the items from coming, but we can learn to observe them as they come and go.

WILL MINDFULNESS HELP ME RELAX?

Another common assumption about mindfulness meditation is that it should result in a greater feeling of relaxation or calmness. Although people who practice mindfulness meditation can feel less stressed, anxious, or depressed as a result of engaging in it, this isn't the underlying intention of meditation. Remember that mindfulness is a way of *paying attention,* and at times, you may notice feelings of tension, stress, anxiety, or another emotional state that isn't relaxation. The goal is to experience these emotions without judgement, not to force them out and induce relaxation. That being said, if we can cultivate more acceptance for a variety of different emotional states, that can often help us feel more at peace and better able to weather emotional storms.

I KEEP FALLING ASLEEP DURING MY MINDFULNESS PRACTICE. IS THIS OKAY?

Many people report feeling sleepy and may doze off during a mindfulness practice, which is understandable, especially if you're closing your eyes and lying down (doesn't this just invite a catnap?). If we return to the idea of what mindfulness is—heightened awareness and acceptance of your present moment experience—you may want to practice mindfulness meditation in contexts and times when you're less likely to fall asleep. If midmorning is a better time, plan to do a guided meditation then. You can also sit up or stand for your meditative practice to help prevent you from falling asleep.

BEING MINDFUL IS DIFFICULT. WILL I GET BETTER AT IT WITH TIME?

There's no denying that paying attention to the present moment is challenging. Our minds bounce around to many different thoughts, including worry, rumination, anticipation, planning, hopes, and fears. That's completely normal and part of the experience of having a human brain—it's always working. Therefore, it's not necessarily the case that our brains get less busy the more we practice mindfulness. It is more that we relate to our thoughts and feelings differently and can shift the spotlight of our attention. When it comes to mindfulness meditation, it is best to think of it as a practice that we engage in for practice sake. It's not a skill to become an expert or even good at. That may be a real paradigm shift for some people. Learning to notice your thoughts and feelings without an agenda to stop, change, or otherwise control them can end up feeling liberating for many.

BRINGING THINGS TOGETHER

You've learned a variety of CBT strategies so far that initially focused on changing the content of your thoughts and altering behaviors to help reduce feelings of anxiety and depression. In this chapter, the focus has been on acknowledging aspects of our lives where change isn't always possible and where acceptance is needed. Acceptance is especially important as we grow older, given the number of things we experience that we won't be able to change, including the death of a spouse, medical diagnoses, reduced mobility or functionality, changes in cognitive functioning, and ultimately our own mortality. On a smaller scale, many of the thoughts and emotions we experience on a daily basis benefit from acceptance.

Acceptance involves an acknowledgement (of thoughts, feelings, or a situation) without judgement and willingness to work with what is offered in the present moment. It doesn't mean we have to like what's happening to us or surrender to it. Acceptance means we stop fighting with what is and work with it in whatever way we can. We can cultivate acceptance by using mental imagery (imagine those party guests), the RAIN process, or a regular mindfulness meditation practice. In practicing to accept instead of avoid, suppress, or deny our experiences, we can be more fully present in our own lives. It doesn't mean we get rid of the pain we experience, but we can learn to exist with pain such that it doesn't turn into suffering. That may be the best gift to give ourselves.

TAKE-HOME POINTS

• Many aspects of our lives as we grow older can't be changed or aren't under our total control. That often creates emotional pain and stress.

• Acceptance is an acknowledgment of what is occurring in the present moment and a willingness to work with it, as opposed to against it.

• Acceptance is not easy, nor does it require us to approve of, or surrender to, something.

• Acceptance can be cultivated by using mental imagery, the RAIN process, and mindfulness meditation.

PUTTING CBT INTO PRACTICE

Over the coming week, identify an area of your life that needs acceptance. It could be an emotional reaction that you have, an automatic thought you experience, or an aspect of a situation (for example, waiting in line or discomfort after physical exercise). Try out one or more of the strategies presented in this chapter. Make some notes about your experience in the Practicing Acceptance Worksheet below and what you learned. Additional copies of this worksheet are available at http://www.newharbin ger.com/51260.

Practicing Acceptance Worksheet Example

Situation to Accept	Mental Imagery	RAIN	Mindfulness	What Did I Experience? What Did I Learn?
Felt pain in hip after doing physical exercise		X		Recognized frustration and annoyance Allowed these feelings Investigated where I felt them (tension in jaw) Nurtured myself by saying "I'm here for you. It's okay to feel this way" Put heating pad on my hip

Practicing Acceptance Worksheet

Situation to Accept	Mental Imagery	RAIN	Mindfulness	What Did I Experience? What Did I Learn?

CHAPTER 10

Maintaining Your Progress and Preventing a Relapse

- *Despite the benefits of CBT, relapses can happen due to the nature of anxiety and depression.*
- *It is possible to prevent or mitigate the impact of relapses by planning ahead.*
- *Relapse-prevention planning consists of identifying the CBT interventions that have been most helpful, distinguishing early warning signs and signs of a relapse or lapse, and setting goals for the future to keep you on track.*
- *You can maintain your progress by regularly checking in with yourself to monitor areas of concern, taking care of your physical health, and ensuring you have adequate social support.*

Congratulations! You've taken a full tour of the CBT landscape and have learned a whole host of strategies to help reduce feelings of anxiety and depression—and live the best life you possibly can as you grow older. As we near the end of this book, you may be noticing some areas of improvement in your life or feel like you are on your way to making meaningful changes in your life. The purpose of this chapter is to reflect on and summarize progress or changes you've made thus far and think ahead to future challenges and ways to be proactive in how you deal with them.

When people are feeling better, the last thing they usually want to think about is the possibility of relapsing, meaning, the return of their symptoms. We know from a large body of research, however, that if people experience an episode of anxiety or depression, there is a reasonable chance that they will experience another (Buckman et al. 2018; Lorimer et al. 2021). The risk of relapse is higher for individuals who have additional mental health difficulties on top of anxiety or depression (for example, substance-use issues, eating disorders, or trauma-related disorders) (Buckman et al. 2018; Lorimer et al. 2021), as well as those with a history of early-life adversity (Buckman et al. 2018). Experiencing a major life stressor or change can also increase risk for a relapse (Lorimer et al. 2021). Given that growing older is full of unexpected changes and challenges, these events can reactivate difficulties with anxiety and depression.

Instead of being surprised by relapses, it's better to be thoughtful about how to reduce the risk of them happening and how you might mitigate the severity of relapses. It is possible to reduce your risk of relapse and catch symptoms early enough to prevent a relapse altogether or stop symptoms from getting worse. The good news is, you've already done a lot to prevent future episodes of anxiety and depression by learning about CBT and practicing new habits. Research suggests this is one the best things you can be doing to prevent your risk of relapse (Zhang et al. 2018). You can further help reduce your risk of sliding backwards by creating a relapse-prevention plan for yourself. This chapter will help you do just that and create a strategy for maintaining your progress.

REFLECTING ON PROGRESS

It's helpful to start by thinking about changes you've witnessed in yourself since starting the book. Not only does this feel satisfying and provide a sense of accomplishment, but it also reminds you that change is possible. You can take steps to help improve how you feel and the quality of your life.

Progress can come in many shapes and forms. It doesn't necessarily need to be a dramatic change in your life. Even small-scale changes can be impactful. Let's say that as part of behavioral activation for depression, you've gotten out for a fifteen-minute walk every other day compared to once a week. Not only does this triple the amount of physical exercise you get (and improve your physical health), but it also significantly boosts mood both during and after the walks. For something that seems relatively small, the cumulative effects can be large. We tend to underestimate the impact of making small changes on our lives, so it's important not to sweep any kind of progress under the rug—especially because changing can be so challenging.

Let's look at some examples of progress made by the characters introduced in the book to help inspire you to think about the changes you've made.

Tina's progress:

- More relaxed visits with grandkids
- Less time spent reviewing finances
- Better quality of sleep at night

Fred's progress:

- Attended two social gatherings alone
- Taking on fewer unnecessary projects at work
- Sharing more personal details with others

Alice's progress:

- No longer avoiding TV shows about cancer
- Calling son less with health worries
- Worrying less about health

Jim's progress:

- Reengaged in physical exercise

- Decreased panic attack frequency by 50 percent
- Went to movie in a theater and didn't leave when feeling anxious

Victor's progress:

- Eating breakfast most days
- More communicative with daughter about their relationship
- Not sleeping as much during the day

Now it's your turn to reflect on areas of progress you've made while working through the book. It may be helpful to look back at the goals you identified in chapter 4 and reflect on the progress you've made toward them. Keep in mind that even if you haven't entirely reached these goals, that's completely normal. Change takes time, and this may just be the start of your efforts to improve your mental health. If you're feeling like you can't identify many changes or signs of improvement, don't forget that making your way through this book is progress. You could just have easily stopped halfway, thrown the book out, or used it to start a bonfire.

Write down some of the progress that you've made toward your goals.

My progress: _____

PREVENTING A RELAPSE

As we've mentioned, if an older adult has experienced an episode of anxiety or depression, the likelihood of them experiencing another one is considerable. Experiencing a significant life change or stressor can be one cause of a relapse. Being diagnosed with a medical issue, relocating to a long-term care facility, or losing a spouse or significant other are all examples of life changes that could potentially cause an episode of anxiety and depression. Changes in medication treatment, lack of access to psychological treatment, or poor response to psychological or pharmacological treatment can also increase risk of relapse.

All this being said, relapses aren't inevitable. It is possible that with early detection of your symptoms and warning signs, you can take action to prevent your symptoms from worsening. This is, in essence, the rationale for developing a relapse-prevention plan. It helps you catch the signs of a symptom lapse early enough that you can potentially prevent a full relapse from occurring.

There are several components of a relapse prevention plan: identifying your CBT strategies; recognizing early warning signs, symptom lapses, and relapses; and setting future goals to stay on track. Let's go through each in a little more detail.

IDENTIFYING YOUR CBT STRATEGIES

In your relapse-prevention plan, clearly list the CBT strategies you've learned and how they have been useful to you. This is a summary of the tools you've compiled in your tool kit. You can think of this as your CBT arsenal. Considering going back to previous chapters to help remind you of some of the strategies. Having them written down can make it easier remember what to do if you notice early warning signs or signs of a lapse or relapse. Let's look at examples from Tina, Jim, and Victor.

Tina's CBT strategies:

- Writing out thoughts, feelings, behaviors, and physical sensations
- Doing situational exposures to help cut back on checking and planning
- Learning to change worries by questioning thoughts

- Engaging in problem-solving for worries about husband's care
- Practicing RAIN when faced with situations outside her control
- Regular mindfulness meditation

Jim's CBT strategies:

- Writing out thoughts, feelings, behaviors, and physical sensations when panic attacks occur
- Changing thoughts about what panic attacks mean and don't mean
- Setting small goals for reengaging in activities avoided because of panic attacks
- Engaging in interoceptive and situational exposures to target feared physical sensations and situations
- Using mindfulness meditation to help accept uncomfortable physical sensations
- Referring back to decisional balance when feeling less motivated to face fears

Victor's CBT strategies:

- Recording thoughts, emotions, behaviors, and physical sensations throughout the day and noticing patterns in mood
- Setting small goals each day for behavioral activation

- Look at decisional balance when he feels like isolating himself
- Engaging in problem-solving for stressors related to daughter
- Use mental imagery to help accept thoughts that he can't change
- Catching and changing thoughts that seem distorted

Now it's your turn. List what CBT strategies have been most helpful to you thus far.

_____

_____

_____

_____

RECOGNIZING EARLY WARNING SIGNS, SYMPTOM LAPSES, AND RELAPSES

To help illustrate the difference between earning warning signs, symptom lapses, and relapses, consider the metaphor of canoeing down a river. On a typical day, it's smooth sailing with a few wildlife sightings and feeling the warm sun on your face. You're paddling along when suddenly you start to hear the sound of rushing water. You quickly recognize that sound is a waterfall and, like the expert canoer you are, take swift action to turn the canoe around. It is significantly harder to turn your canoe around when you're at the tip of the waterfall or halfway down. Turning your canoe around when you hear rushing water is the equivalent of identifying early warning signs of your anxiety and depression. Recognizing early indicators that your symptoms are worsening gives you the best chance of intervening and preventing a lapse or relapse.

Early warning signs, symptom lapses, and relapses differ in degree and severity. While an early warning sign for Victor could be missing two of his grandson's soccer games in a row, a symptom lapse could be missing a week's worth of games, and a relapse could be missing playoff season altogether. Making this distinction helps us recognize differences in the severity of our symptoms and can guide what type of help we need. For example, if Victor has had a relapse and his metaphorical canoe is at the bottom of the waterfall, he may need help from his family doctor and individual therapy from a mental health professional.

One other important reason for distinguishing early warning signs from symptom lapses and relapses has to do with how we deal with bad days. Sometimes we have the tendency to catastrophize bad days or think in black-and-white about them, for example, *I was irritable today—my depression must be back again.* The reality is that we will all have bad days, and if we can keep these days in healthy perspective, this can prevent bad days from turning into early warning signs, symptom lapses, or relapses.

As you start to consider whether you're dealing with early warning signs, a symptoms lapse, or a relapse, there are a few helpful guidelines to keep in mind.

- Try to keep your focus on *specific behaviors* that are indicators of early warning signs, a symptom lapse, or a relapse. This helps us recognize them more easily compared to focusing on emotions as early warning signs. Avoiding driving on the highway is a more helpful early warning sign then feeling anxious about driving.

- Specify how much or how often a behavior occurs in order for it to be problematic. This allows you to more easily recognize when something is a problem. Calling your son twice a day to seek reassurance when you feel anxious is a good example of this.

- Think about what behaviors you were doing *more* or *less* of when you were at your worst. Think back to when you were most depressed or anxious. What were you doing differently at that time? Perhaps you weren't getting any physical exercise or doing very little. Maybe you were overcommitting yourself to various activities and not allowing enough time for relaxation or downtime.

With these parameters in mind, try to identify your early warning signs, and signs of a lapse and relapse. For more inspiration, review the lists created by Fred and Alice.

Fred's list:

- Early warning signs: Saying no to two social invites in a week due to anxiety, taking on one or more additional projects at work despite having a full workload
- Signs of a lapse: Saying no to most social invites in a two-week period due to anxiety, taking on two or more additional projects at work despite having a full workload
- Signs of a relapse: Saying no to all social invites in a two-week period due to anxiety, saying yes to all additional projects at work despite having a full workload

Alice's list:

- Early warning signs: Calling son twice in a week to ask for reassurance about health worries, avoiding watching a TV or movie with mention of cancer once in three weeks
- Signs of a lapse: Calling son three times in a week to ask for reassurance about health

worries, avoiding watching a TV show or movie with mention of cancer two to three times a month

- Signs of a relapse: Calling son every day to ask for reassurance about health worries, avoiding watching a TV or movie with mention of cancer whenever possible

Now it's your turn to identify your early warning signs and signs of a lapse and relapse.

Early warning signs: _____

_____

_____

Signs of a lapse: _____

_____

_____

Signs of a relapse: _____

_____

_____

SETTING GOALS FOR THE FUTURE

We spoke at length in chapter 4 about the importance of setting goals as you engage in CBT, and we return to that idea in the context of relapse prevention. Continuing to set goals for the future can help you stay on track and further reduce your anxiety or depression. Making progress toward goals is positively reinforcing and further motivates your efforts to keep up with your CBT strategies. So, take a few moments to reflect on goals that you're continuing to work toward or new goals that you'd like to achieve in the future. Examples of Victor's and Tina's future goals are provided below.

Victor's future goals:

- Take a cooking class
- Volunteer at grandson's school
- Start a vegetable garden in backyard

Tina's future goals:

- Have grandkids over for a weekend sleepover
- Take more time for myself away from my husband (for example, go for lunch with a friend)
- Allow myself to spend money on pleasurable things (for example, going for a massage)

Now it's your turn to write down goals that you're continuing to work toward or new goals that you'd like to achieve in the future.

Future goals: _____

MAINTAINING PROGRESS

As you think about preventing a relapse and continue to set goals for the future, you may be wondering what you can do more broadly to maintain any gains that you've made and stay on a positive trajectory. In this section, we have several recommendations to help you maintain any progress you've made in your CBT journey to date.

Check in with Yourself

You give time, energy, and effort to the things that matter most in your life, such as your physical health, family and friends, or hobbies. The same applies when it comes to taking care of your mental health. It requires regular tending much like a garden would, and this tending can vary from person to person. Your mental health *maintenance* may look different than other peoples'. One important habit for anyone, however, is setting an appointment with yourself once a week to do a mental health check-in. You can use the questions below to help guide these efforts. By answering the questions in the Checking in with Myself Worksheet, you can remain aware of how you're feeling and prompt yourself to be proactive about managing your anxiety or depression. (Additional copies of this worksheet are available at http://www.newharbin

ger.com/51260.) See examples of these questions completed by Fred below.

Checking In with Myself: Fred

How has my week been?

Good overall

I made a point of talking more with my neighbor

My wife is upset with me because I've been staying late at work to finish projects

I felt mildly anxious before meeting some new friends for dinner

---

What emotions, thoughts, behaviors, or physical sensations have I noticed?

Emotions: Anxiety, guilt

Thoughts: I should be finishing everything I need to in the workday. What if our new friends think I'm socially anxious?

Behaviors: Staying late at work, getting defensive with my wife, having a glass of wine before going out for dinner

Physical sensations: Some tension in upper back

What, if anything, is concerning about the emotions, thoughts, or behaviors I observed?

Some cognitive distortions in my thoughts

Staying late at work doesn't really help my anxiety

Getting defensive with wife just makes things more difficult for both of us

---

Is there anything from CBT I can implement to help to cope with what I observed this week?

Practice questioning and changing my thoughts

Situational exposures

Acceptance

Problem-solving

Disclose to wife how I'm feeling and what support would be helpful from her

---

What specific homework can I set for myself this week?

Dedicate fifteen minutes to writing down my thoughts, then questioning and changing them

Do exposures: Leave work on time each day, follow up with new friends over the phone

Limit alcohol before social gatherings

Practice accepting the discomfort that I feel during exposures

Engage in problem-solving for how I can scale back at work

Checking In with Myself Worksheet

How has my week been?

What emotions, thoughts, behaviors, or physical sensations have I noticed?

Emotions:

Thoughts:

Behaviors:

Physical sensations:

What, if anything, is concerning about the emotions, thoughts, or behaviors I observed?

Is there anything from CBT I can implement to help to cope with what I observed this week?

What specific homework can I set for myself this week?

TAKING CARE OF PHYSICAL NEEDS

Another important consideration in maintaining progress is your physical health. It can be easy to see our physical needs as separate from our emotional world, but they are indeed intimately connected. Things like sleep, diet, and exercise all have a direct impact on how we feel emotionally as well as on our ability to think clearly and behave in ways that help us reach our goals. Let's examine some aspects of our physicality and how meeting (or failing to meet) our physical needs influences anxiety and depression.

Sleep

If the average person sleeps eight hours a night, they will spend approximately a third of their life asleep. The amount of time we spend asleep in our lives reflects the tremendous importance of dozing off. We all know that sleep helps us rest and recharge for the next day, but there are a whole host of other ways in which sleep is critical for our physical and emotional health. Getting adequate sleep enables us to problem-solve, reason, pay attention to detail, and regulate our moods. Just ask parents of a young infant to tell you about the impact of sleep on how they think and feel. They may tell you they have a hard time concentrating, are tearful, or feel irritable or short-tempered. Cognition and emotion aside, sleep impacts a multitude of other life-sustaining systems in our bodies, including our immune system, appetite, growth and stress hormones, blood pressure, and cardiovascular health.

Given sleep's many benefits, getting your recommended seven to nine hours per night is a no-brainer. But adults can experience reduced quality and quantity of sleep as they get older, unfortunately. Part of this is due to changes and disruptions to your circadian rhythm, the twenty-four-hour cycle our bodies run on. As a result, older adults may find themselves getting up earlier in the morning and being more tired earlier in the day (for example, early afternoon). They may nap to compensate, which can further disrupt sleep at night. Difficulties with sleep in late life can also be due to physical pain, medical conditions (for example, nighttime urination or sleep apnea), or medications. This can result in awaking more frequently and feeling less rested in the morning.

Some of the most important things you can do to improve your sleep hygiene in late life are:

- Have a consistent bedtime and wake time every day. Older adults can have more difficulty recovering from lost sleep and variable sleep schedules. Try to stick to the same bedtime and wake time each day.
- Use your bed only for sleeping. It can be tempting to treat your bed as a second couch or home office, but as best that you can, restrict your time and activities in bed to sleeping only. This also means getting up and out of bed if you are sleepless for longer

than thirty minutes. Go lie down somewhere comfortable and engage in a relaxing activity (for example, listen to calming music).

- Limit naps during the day. As much as you might feel drowsy during the early to mid-afternoon hours, try to keep napping to a minimum. This will help keep your circadian rhythm on track and allow you to sleep at night.
- Try to get daily exercise and light exposure. Physical exercise is one of the best things you can do for your overall health and sleep hygiene. Even a little bit can go a long way. Light exposure, particularly in the morning hours, also helps regulate your circadian rhythm and get better quality of sleep.
- Limit substances that disrupt sleep. This can include alcohol, caffeine, or over-the-counter sleep medications. Also consider refraining from eating large meals four hours before bedtime.

If there are any changes you wish to make to your sleep hygiene, list them here.

Diet

Think of the last time when you went too long between meals. Aside from your stomach growling, what else did you feel or notice at the time? Chances are, you weren't feeling at your best. The popularized term "hangry" appropriately captures the anger that sits close to the surface when you feel hungry.

Consuming regular, well-balanced meals and snacks is essential in order to keep our bodies and brains in good working order and by extension, keeping our emotional lives as stable as they can be. Older adults can experience a decline in appetite as they age for a multitude of reasons, including hormonal changes, reduced physical activity, changes in taste or smell, issues with swallowing or teeth, and illnesses such as Alzheimer's Disease or cancer. Older adults who live alone may also be less inclined to prepare meals or enjoy eating given that meals are often a social activity. Reduced appetites can lead to unintentional weight loss and reduction of muscle mass in older adults. This can lead to physical health issues and increased risk for falls and injuries.

The message here is a pretty simple one: do what you can to consume regular, well-balanced meals and snacks. Try to keep to a regular schedule of eating as opposed to waiting until you feel ravenous (which may result in overeating). Consider consuming small but more frequent portions of more nutrient- and calorically dense food, such as avocado, nuts or nut butters, eggs, olive oil, full-fat milk, or cheese. Try to keep easy-to-eat food and snacks readily available, including when you're on outings. If chewing is a problem for you, consider smoothies or milkshakes. Keeping your body fed means you feed your brain and give yourself a better chance of regulating your emotions.

If there are any changes you wish to make to your diet, list them here.

Exercise

We've all been told that getting regular exercise is important for our physical and mental health (Rector, Richter & Lerman 2019). There's no shortage of research supporting the benefits on older adults' strength, aerobic capacity, flexibility, and physical function (Keysor & Jette 2001). But what benefits does it confer for mental health in late life? A large body of research suggests that regular physical exercise for older adults can significantly reduce symptoms of depression (Klil-Drori et al. 2020) and anxiety

(Chong et al. 2022) and improve cognitive functioning (Middleton et al. 2008; Neviani et al. 2017).

For all the good that exercise can do for older adults, there are a whole host of barriers that can get in the way of being physically active. Acute or chronic illness, disability, or mobility issues, for example, can make it much more challenging to get physical exercise in late life. Other barriers can be motivation and lack of access to resources needed for exercise. The good news is: you don't have to adopt an extensive, complicated, or overly vigorous physical activity regimen to benefit from it. The U.S. Department of Health and Human Services recommends that older adults participate in moderate-intensity aerobic activity for at least thirty minutes on five days of the week, or vigorous-intensity aerobic activity for at least twenty minutes on three days of the week. Consult with your physician before starting new physical activity and work with a trusted health advisor to develop a safe, effective, and fun workout routine work to limit risk of injury.

If the above recommendations feel beyond the scope of what you currently do or can do, consider setting some smaller, more gradual goals for physical exercise that fit within the scope of what you currently do and your physical capabilities. For example, park a little farther away from the shopping mall to get additional steps in or lift weights while sitting down. A little bit can go a long way when it comes to getting physical exercise in late life.

If there are any changes you wish to make with respect to physical exercise, list them here.

CONNECTING WITH OTHERS

Along with self-check-ins and taking care of physical needs, a final consideration to help maintain your progress has to do with your connection to other people. We are social creatures who very much need the company, support, and companionship of others in order to survive and thrive. Social support is widely recognized as a strong protective factor for anxiety and depression, and that is very much the case in late life. Your community can include friends, family members, a spouse, your religious or spiritual community, health care providers, and casual acquaintances, such as the regulars at your local coffee shop.

It's not necessarily the size of one's community that matters but rather the quality of the relationships you have with people. In his book *Loneliness,* the psychologist John Cacioppo highlights that it's more important that we have at least one person in your life who you feel you can be yourself with and who you feel understands and cares for you (2009).

Reflect on and write down who you consider to be the supportive person(s) in your life. If you can't identify a main support person, see if you can identify people you'd like to deepen your existing relationship with.

TAKE-HOME POINTS

- *CBT can help reduce your risk of relapses. By creating a relapse-prevention plan you can help prevent or mitigate the impact of symptom lapses or relapses.*

- *Your relapse-prevention plan includes listing CBT strategies that have been helpful to you, identifying early warning signs and signs of a lapse or relapse, and setting future goals.*

- *You can maintain your progress by engaging in regular self-check-ins, looking after your physical needs, and remaining connected to the supportive people in your life.*

PUTTING CBT INTO PRACTICE

Refer to the components of your relapse-prevention plan that you recorded in this chapter as often as you need. Continue to use the Checking in with Myself worksheet below to reflect regularly (aim for weekly) on how you're doing and to stay on top of your progress. You can download additional copies of the worksheet at http://www.newharbinger.com/51260.

Checking In with Myself Worksheet

How has my week been?

What emotions, thoughts, behaviors, or physical sensations have I noticed?
Emotions:
Thoughts:
Behaviors:
Physical sensations:

What, if anything, is concerning about the emotions, thoughts, or behaviors I observed?

Is there anything from CBT I can implement to help to cope with what I observed this week?

What specific homework can I set for myself this week?

WHAT'S NEXT?

- *We conclude the book with final thoughts about mental health in late life, how we maximize our final years of life, and where to go next in your mental health journey.*

Conclusion

As we conclude the *Aging Well Workbook,* we'd like to highlight a few remaining topics to help prepare you for the next chapter of your life and continue your journey to improve your mental health.

But first, take a moment to give yourself a gigantic pat on the back for reading this book and actively participating in learning and implementing CBT strategies. It is often far easier to continue on as per usual than it is to take steps to change and persist in doing so. Congratulations!

Remind yourself of all that you've learned. You've acquired a lot of information about what CBT is and how it attempts to help people improve their mental health. You've learned about the nature of anxiety and sadness and how these emotions provide us with information and motivate us to take action. You've also become aware of when anxiety and sadness become disordered and the symptoms of different anxiety disorders and clinical depression in older adults. You've learned about the value of goal-setting in CBT and how to set goals that you can actually achieve. You've engaged in self-monitoring of your symptoms—highlighting the interrelationship between your thoughts, feelings, behaviors, and physical sensations. That increased self-awareness was important as you then learned how to change your thinking—a fundamental skill to help you cope when anxiety and depression causes you to think in extremes.

Let's not forget how you learned how to boost your mood and conquer your anxiety by doing behavioral activation and exposure therapy, respectively. These are two interventions that will help you maximize the quality of your life moving forward. Then you learned how to engage in a structured process of problem-solving to help tackle the challenges of growing older. For other challenges that require acceptance, you learned what this means (and doesn't mean) and several different ways of coming to terms with what can't be changed. Finally, you took relapse prevention into your own hands and made a plan for how to stay on track with any progress that you've made.

That's a lot of ground you've covered. Well done! Aside from acquiring a considerable amount of new information and practicing new ways of coping with anxiety and depression, you have demonstrated that you are willing and open to learning ways of bettering yourself—no small feat after a lifetime of practicing certain ways of thinking and behaving.

LIVING A MEANINGFUL LIFE AS YOU AGE

Using CBT-based strategies can be situated within broader efforts to live a meaningful life in your later adult years. What exactly makes for a meaningful life in older adulthood? Philosophers and social scientists alike have long attempted to answer this question, and there appear to be some recurring themes in their answers.

Living a life with meaning and purpose can emerge, in part, from engaging in things that are consistent with your values. Knowing what your values are is an important first step in this process. Some examples are service to others, friendship, personal growth, independence, family, health, creativity, and spirituality. You may wish to spend a few moments identifying what your most important values are. After doing so, you may be better situated to prioritize things that honor your values. Doing what is important to us, whether that's experiencing new countries and cultures, keeping up a regular exercise routine, or maintaining certain traditions with your grandkids, is one important component of living a life of meaning and purpose.

It's hard to imagine a life that feels meaningful without the presence of other people we love and who love us in return. Having supportive relationships tends to be one of the strongest predictors of life satisfaction no matter what age you are. Not only do relationships feel satisfying and rewarding, but they also tend to buffer us from life's many ups and downs. It can become easier to weather life's many storms when you have people around you who you feel will be there for you when you need it. Vice versa, it can feel meaningful to support others when they go through challenging times. If you are feeling lacking in social support at this time in your life, you may be feeling sad, lonely, or vulnerable. It can feel daunting to try to improve close relationships as you get older and you might even feel that your prospects of doing so are limited. Know that you are not alone. You might consider choosing one person who is a looser social connection (for example, an acquaintance from a workout class) you'd like to deepen your friendship with or alternatively making an effort to connect more frequently, for example, on social media, with your closest loved ones and friends. Taking small steps to deepen a relationship often can go a long way.

One additional consideration when it comes to living a meaningful life in older adulthood (although there are many more we could highlight) relates to the idea of agency. The ability to make choices and exert agency over important aspects of our life is a fundamental human need. You need to only think to a time in your life when your agency or sense of control was limited (for example, being physically injured, not being able to drive, or job loss) to realize how important this is to our psychological and emotional well-being. Late adulthood be a time when your perceived agency changes. With changes in physical health, cognition, mobility, or functional ability, it can start to feel like you have less control over your life and what happens to you. This can be downright scary. As difficult as it can be to not have control over things that you used to, it's important to shift your focus to the things that you still can control. If your memory is failing you, try getting creative with memory aids (for example, visual cues, audio reminders, or mnemonic devices) and rely more on others to help compensate. If you are no longer able to drive, turning to friends who can or arranging for alternative transportation are good options to focus on. Focusing on what you can control as opposed to what you can't, as difficult as it can be sometimes, will help you be resilient and continue to live meaningful life as you grow older.

CONTINUING YOUR JOURNEY

This book may just be the start of your journey to improving your mental health in late life. It can be difficult to know where to go next and what you need. Here's a few next steps to consider:

Individual or Group Therapy

Consider this option if you need additional assistance carrying out the interventions discussed in this book or have other types of mental health issues that are need of more intensive support (for example, OCD, substance-use issues, or bipolar disorder). You can consult organizations such as the Association for Behavioral and Cognitive Therapies (http://www.abct.org) or the Canadian Association for Cognitive Behavioural Therapy (http://www.cacbt.ca) for more information about where to find CBT therapists near you.

Medication Treatment

Pharmacological treatment can be of significant help to individuals who may not be benefiting from CBT as much as they could because of the severity of their symptoms. Antidepressant medications are a safe and effective therapy alongside CBT for older adults (Wetherell et al. 2013). Geriatric psychiatrists are medical doctors with specialized training in treating mental disorders that occur in late life. If available, consider arranging a consultation with a geriatric psychiatrist and if not accessible, a general psychiatrist or family physician may also be able to help you.

Other Health Professionals

You may need the help of other health professionals if you're dealing with other stressors associated with aging, such as reduced mobility, a physical injury, difficulties eating or swallowing, or cognitive decline. Consider how other health professionals, such as an occupational therapist, social worker, physiotherapist, registered dietician, or speech language pathologist, may be needed for your concerns. Getting help for these issues can have a positive impact on your mental health.

Peer Support

Sharing your struggles with others who have similar concerns can be very valuable and therapeutic. There are a variety of peer support organizations for individuals with mental health concerns, where you can both discuss your issues and support others who may be going through something similar. Organizations will vary depending on where you reside. If you're in the United States or Canada, consider exploring your options by visiting one of these websites:

- Mental Health America (http://www.mhanatio nal.org/find-support-groups)
- Peer Support Canada (http://www.peersuppor tcanada.ca)

Helpful Organizations

There are a variety of organizations devoted to supporting older adults with anxiety or depression. This support can include, for example, information about mental disorders and treatment, links to community or online resources, and advocating on behalf of older adults with mental health difficulties. The organizations listed below offer a range of supports, both specific to older adults and for all ages.

- American Association for Geriatric Psychiatry (http://www.gmhfonline.org)
- Anxiety and Depression Association of America (http://www.adaa.org)
- Association for Behavioral and Cognitive Therapies (http://www.abct.org)
- National Coalition on Mental Health and Aging (http://www.ncmha.org)
- National Institute of Mental Health (http://www.nimh.nih.gov)

  These organizations are based in Canada:

- Anxiety Canada (http://www.anxietycanada.com)
- Canadian Association of Cognitive and Behavioural Therapies (http://www.cacbt.ca)
- Canadian Coalition for Seniors' Mental Health (http://www.ccsmh.ca)
- Canadian Mental Health Association (http://www.cmha.ca)

- Mood Disorders Society of Canada (http://w ww.mdsc.ca)

BEST OF LUCK ON YOUR JOURNEY

At the end of this journey, another exciting one awaits you. We wish you all the success in making your later adult years as rewarding and gratifying as possible. We'll leave you with an important reminder from author C.S. Lewis, "You can't go back and change the beginning, but you can start where you are and change the ending."

Acknowledgements

Thank you to our older adult clients who never cease to inspire us with their resilience and humble us with their wisdom.

We would like to express our gratitude to the editorial team at New Harbinger for their enthusiasm for the book and guidance in the writing process. Thank you to Robert Leahy for graciously agreeing to write the foreword.

JE would like to thank Neil Rector, Corey Mackenzie, Judith Laposa, and Donna Akman for their mentorship, support, and always setting the bar high for clinical psychologists. Many thanks to family members, friends, and colleagues for their support and encouragement.

NAR would like to acknowledge Aaron T. Beck for his profound contributions to the reduction of human suffering and the modeling of positive aging through to centenarian status.

References

American Psychiatric Association. (2013). *Diagnostic and Statistical Manual of Mental Disorders* (5th ed). Arlington, VA: APA.

Balsamo, M., F. Cataldi, L. Carlucci, & B. Fairfield. (2018). Assessment of Anxiety in Older Adults: A Review of Self-Report Measures. *Clinical Interventions in Aging* 13: 573–93.

Bakker, D., & N. Rickard. (2018). Engagement in Mobile Phone App for Self-Monitoring of Emotional Well-Being Predicts Changes in Mental Health: MoodPrism. *Journal of Affective Disorders* 227: 432–442.

Beck, A., A.J. Rush, B.F. Shaw, & G. Emery. (1979). *Cognitive Therapy of Depression.* New York: Guilford Press.

Blair, S.N., & W.L. Haskell. (2006). Objectively Measured Physical Activity and Mortality in Older Adults. *Journal of the American Medical Association* 296: 216–218.

Brach, T. (2020). *Radical Compassion: Learning to Love Yourself and Your World with the Practice of RAIN*. New York: Penguin Life.

Buckman, J.E.J., A. Underwood, K. Clarke, R. Saunders, S.D. Hollon, P. Fearon, & S. Pilling. (2018). Risk Factors for Relapse and Recurrence of Depression in Adults and How They Operate: A Four-Phase Systematic Review and Meta-Synthesis. *Clinical Psychology Review* 64: 13–38.

Button, M.L., H.A. Westra, K.M. Hara, & A. Aviram. (2015). Disentangling the Impact of Resistance and Ambivalence on Therapy Outcomes on Cognitive Behavioral Therapy for Generalized Anxiety Disorder. *Cognitive Behavioral Therapy* 44: 44–53.

Burns, D.D. (1980). *Feeling Good: The New Mood Therapy*. New York: Signet.

Cacioppo, J., & W. Patrick. (2009). *Loneliness: Human Nature and the Need for Connection*. New York: W.W. Norton.

Carstensen, L.L., & M. DeLiema. (2018). The Positivity Effect: A Negativity Bias in Youth Fades with Age. *Current Opinion in Behavioural Science* 19: 7–12.

Carstensen, L.L., & J.A. Mikels. (2005). At the Intersection of Emotion and Cognition: Aging and the Positivity Effect. *Current Directions in Psychological Science* 14: 117–121.

Charles, S.T., C.A. Reynolds, & M. Gatz. (2001). Age-Related Differences and Change in Positive and Negative Affect over 23 Years. *Journal of Personality and Social Psychology* 80: 136–151.

Christensen, H., A.F. Jorm, A. Mackinnon, A. Korten, P. Jacomb, A. Henderson, et al. (1999). Age Differences in Depression and Anxiety Symptoms: A Structural Equation Modelling Analysis of Data from a General Population Sample. *Psychological Medicine* 29: 325–339.

Chong, T.W.H., S. Kootar, H. Wilding, S. Berriman, E. Curran, K.L. Cox, et al. (2022). Exercise Interventions to Reduce Anxiety in Mid-Life and Late-Life Anxiety Disorders and Subthreshold Anxiety Disorder: A Systematic Review. *Therapeutic Advances in Psychopharmacology* 12.

Conwell, Y., & C. Thompson. (2008). Suicidal Behavior in Elders. *Psychiatric Clinics of North America* 31: 333–356.

Coudin, G., & T. Alexopoulos. (2010). "Help Me? I'm Old?" How Negative Aging Stereotypes Create Dependency Among Older Adults. *Aging and Mental Health* 14: 516–523.

Cruikshank, M. (2003). *Learning to Be Old: Gender, Culture, and Aging.* Lanham, MD: Rowman & Littlefield.

DiMauro, J., J. Domingues, G. Fernandez, & D.F. Tolin. (2013). Long-Term Effectiveness of CBT for Anxiety Disorders in an Adult Outpatient Clinic Sample: A Follow-Up Study. *Behaviour Research and Therapy* 51: 82–86.

Erickson, J. & N.A. Rector. (2022). Anxiety Disorders in Late Life: Considerations for Assessment and Cognitive Behavioral Treatment. *Cognitive and Behavioral Practice* 29: 635–647.

Gould, R.L., M.C. Coulson, & R.J. Howard. (2012a). Cognitive Behavioral Therapy for Anxiety Disorders in Older People: A Meta-Analysis and Meta-Regression of

Randomized Controlled Trials. *Journal of the American Geriatrics Society* 60: 218–229.

Gould, R.L., M.C. Coulson, & R.J. Howard. (2012b). Cognitive Behavioral Therapy for Depression in Older People: A Meta-Analysis and Meta-Regression of Randomized Controlled Trials. *Journal of the American Geriatrics Society* 60: 1817–1830.

Holt-Lunstad, J., T.B. Smith, M. Baker, T. Harris, & D. Stephenson. (2015). Loneliness and Social Isolation as Risk Factors for Mortality: A Meta-Analytic Review. *Perspectives on Psychological Science* 10: 227–237.

Holm, A.L., & E. Severinsson. (2015). Mapping Psychosocial Risk and Protective Factors in Suicidal Older Persons: A Systematic Review. *Open Journal of Nursing* 5: 260–275.

Hughes, T.F., C.C. Chang, J. Vander Bilt, & M. Ganguli. (2010). Engagement in Reading and Hobbies and Risk of Incident Dementia: The MoVIES Project. *American Journal of Alzheimer's Disease* 25: 432–438.

Jamison, K.R. (1997). *An Unquiet Mind: A Memoir of Moods and Madness.* New York: Vintage Books.

Kabat-Zinn, J. (2013). *Full Catastrophe Living.* New York: Bantam.

Kabat-Zinn, J. (2009). *Wherever You Go, There You Are: Mindfulness Meditation in Everyday Life.* New York: Hachette Books.

Kabat-Zinn, J. (1982). An Outpatient Program in Behavioral Medicine for Chronic Pain Patients Based on the Practices of Mindfulness Meditation: Theoretical Considerations and Preliminary Results. *General Hospital Psychiatry* 4: 33–47.

Karlin, B.E., M. Trockel, G.K. Brown, M. Gordienko, J. Yesavage, & C.B. Taylor. (2015). Comparison of the Effectiveness of Cognitive Behavioral Therapy for Depression Among Older Versus Younger Veterans: Results of a National Evaluation. *The Journals of Gerontology: Series B* 70: 3–12.

Kessler, R.C., H. Birnbaum, E. Bromet, I. Hwang, N. Sampson, & V. Shaly. (2010). Age Differences in Major Depression: Results from the National

Comorbidity Surveys Replication (NCS-R). *Psychological Medicine* 40: 225–37.

Kessler, R.C., P.E. Greenberg, K.D. Mickelson, L. Meneades, & P.S. Wang. (2001). The Effects of Chronic Medical Conditions on Work Loss and Work Cutback. *Journal of Occupational and Environmental Medicine* 43: 218–25.

Keysor, J.K., & A.M. Jette. (2001). Have We Oversold the Benefit of Late-Life Exercise? *The Journals of Gerontology: Series A* 56: 412–423.

King, L.A. (2001). The Health Benefits of Writing About Life Goals. *Personality and Social Psychology Bulletin* 27: 798–807.

Klil-Drori, S., A.J. Klil-Drori, S. Pira, & S. Rej. (2020). Exercise Intervention for Late Life Depression: A Meta-Analysis. *Journal of Clinical Psychiatry* 8: 19r12877.

Leahy, R. (2006) *The Worry Cure: Seven Steps to Stop Worry from Stopping You.* New York: Three Rivers Press.

Levy, B.R., J.M. Hausdorff, R. Hencke, & J.Y. Wei. (2000). Reducing Cardiovascular Stress with

Positive Self-Stereotypes of Aging. *The Journal of Gerontology: Series B* 55: 205–213.

Levy, B.R., M.D. Slade, S.R. Kunke, & S.V. Kasl. (2002). Longevity Increased by Positive Self-Perceptions of Aging. *Journal of Personality and Social Psychology* 83: 261–270.

Linehan, M. (2015). *DBT Skills Training Manual* (2nd ed.). New York: Guilford Press.

Lisko, I., J. Kulmala, M. Annetorp, T. Ngandu, F. Mangialashe, & M. Kivipelto. (2021). How Can Dementia and Disability Be Prevented in Older Adults: Where Are We Today and Where Are We Going? *Journal of Internal Medicine* 6: 807–830.

Lorimer, B., S. Kellett, A. Nye, & J. Delgadillo. (2021). Predictors of Relapse and Recurrence Following Cognitive Behavioural Therapy for Anxiety-Related Disorders: A Systematic Review. *Cognitive Behaviour Therapy* 50: 1–18.

Mackenzie, C.S., J. Pagura, & J. Sareen. (2010). Correlates of Perceived Need for and Use of Mental Health Services by Older Adults in the Collaborative Psychiatric Epidemiology Surveys.

Journal of American Geriatric Society 18: 1103–1115.

Middleton, L.E., A. Mitnitski, N. Fallah, S.A. Kirkland, & K. Rockwood. (2008). Changes in Cognition and Mortality in Relation to Exercise in Late Life: A Population-Based Study. *PLOS ONE* 3: e3124.

Moos, R.H., P.L. Brennan, K.K. Schutte, & B.S. Moos. (2010). Older Adults' Health and Late-Life Drinking Patterns: A 20-Year Perspective. *Aging & Mental Health* 14: 33–43.

Neviani, F., M.B. Murri, C. Mussi, F. Triolo, G. Toni, E. Simoncini, et al. (2017). Physical Exercise for Late Life Depression: Effects on Cognition and Disability. *International Psychogeriatrics* 29: 1105–1112.

Norcross, J.C., & D.J. Vangarelli. (1989). The Resolution Solution: Longitudinal Examination of New Year's Change Attempts. *Journal of Substance Abuse* 1: 127–134.

Orsillo, S., & L. Roemer. (2011). *The Mindful Way through Anxiety: Break Free from Chronic Worry and Reclaim Your Life*. New York: Guilford Press.

Palmer, B.W., D.V. Jeste, & J.I. Sheikh. (1997). Anxiety Disorders in the Elderly: DSM-IV and Other Barriers to Diagnosis and Treatment. *Journal of Affective Disorders* 46: 183–190.

Rector, N.A., M.A. Richter, & B. Lerman. (2019). Physical Exercise in the Management of Anxiety Disorders and OCD. In *Lifestyle Psychiatry: Using Exercise, Diet, and Mindfulness to Manage Psychiatric Disorders*, edited by D. Noorday. Washington, DC: APA.

Reynolds, K., R.H. Pietrzak, R. El-Gabalawy, & C.S. Mackenzie. (2015). Prevalence of Psychiatric Disorders in U.S. Older Adults: Findings from a Nationally Representative Survey. *World Psychiatry* 14: 74–81.

Rodda, J., Z. Walker, & J. Carter. (2011). Depression in Older Adults. *British Medical Journal* 343: 683–687.

Rogers, C.R. (1995). *On Becoming a Person: A Therapist's View of Psychotherapy*. Boston: Houghton Mifflin.

Roshanaei-Moghaddam, B., M.C. Pauly, D.C. Atkins, S.A. Baldwin, M.B. Stein, & P. Roy-Byrne. (2011). Relative Effects of CBT and

Pharmacotherapy in Depression Versus Anxiety: Is Medication Somewhat Better for Depression, and CBT Somewhat Better for Anxiety? *Depression & Anxiety* 28: 560–576.

Seeman, T.E., T.M. Lusignolo, M. Albert, & L. Berkman. (2001). Social Relationships, Social Support, and Patterns of Cognitive Aging in Healthy, High-Functioning Older Adults: MacArthur Studies of Successful Aging. *Health Psychology* 20: 243–255.

Shen, W., Y. Zhao, B. Hommel, Y. Yuan, Y. Zhang, Z. Liu, et al. (2019). The Impact of Spontaneous and Induced Mood States on Problem Solving and Memory. *Thinking Skills and Creativity 32:* 66–74.

Tilvis, R.S., V. Laitala, P.E. Routasalo, & K.H. Pitkala. (2011). Suffering from Loneliness Indicates Significant Mortality Risk of Older People. *Journal of Aging Research* 2011: 534781.

Walker, D.A., & M. Clarke. (2001). Cognitive Behavioral Psychotherapy: A Comparison Between Younger and Older Adults in Two Inner City Mental Health Teams. *Aging & Mental Health* 5: 197–199.

Wells, K.B., A. Stewart, R.D. Hays, M.A. Burnam, W. Rogers, M. Daniela, et al. (1989). The Functioning and Well-Being of Depressed Patients: Results from the Medical Outcomes Study. *Journal of the American Medical Association* 262: 914–919.

Wetherell, J.L., A.J. Petkus, K.S. White, H. Nguyen, S. Kornblith, C. Andreescu, et al. (2013). Antidepressant Medication Augmented with Cognitive-Behavioral Therapy for Generalized Anxiety Disorder in Older Adults. *American Journal of Psychiatry* 170: 782–789.

Wiles, N.J., L. Thomas, N. Turner, K. Garfield, D. Kounali, J. Campbell, et al. (2016). Long-Term Effectiveness and Cost-Effectiveness of Cognitive Behavioural Therapy as an Adjunct to Pharmacotherapy for Treatment-Resistant Depression in Primary Care: Follow-Up of the CoBalT Randomised Controlled Trial. *The Lancet Psychiatry* 3: 137–144.

Williams, M., J. Teasdale, Z. Segal, & J. Kabat-Zinn. (2007). *The Mindful Way Through Depression: Freeing Yourself from Chronic Sadness.* New York: Guilford Press.

Wolitsky-Taylor, K.B., N. Castriotta, E. Lenze, M. Stanley, & M.G. Craske. (2010). Anxiety Disorders in Older Adults: A Comprehensive Review. *Depression & Anxiety* 27: 190–211.

Zhang, Z., L. Zhang, G. Zhang, J. Jin, & Z. Zheng. (2018). The Effect of CBT and Its Modifications for Relapse Prevention in Major Depressive Disorder: A Systematic Review and Meta-Analysis. *BMC Psychiatry* 18: 50.

Julie Erickson, PhD, is a clinical psychologist, and adjunct faculty member in the department of applied psychology and human development at the University of Toronto. Erickson's research interests focus on optimizing evidence-based psychological treatment for older adults, and reducing barriers to treatment-seeking. She offers workshops, seminars, and clinical supervision on cognitive behavioral therapy (CBT) with older adults. She maintains an active clinical practice focusing on the treatment of adults across the lifespan. Erickson's research has been published in journals such as *Aging and Mental Health, Depression and Anxiety, Clinical Psychology Review,* and *Cognitive and Behavioral Practice.*

Neil A. Rector, PhD, is a senior research scientist at the Sunnybrook Research Institute (SRI); director of the Mood and Anxiety Research and Treatment Program; and director of research for the Thompson Anxiety Disorder Centre in the department of psychiatry at the Sunnybrook Health Sciences Centre in Toronto, ON, Canada. Rector's research interests focus on the study of cognitive and behavioral mechanisms of vulnerability in the development and persistence of anxiety and mood disorders, and their treatment with CBT. In addition to having an active CBT practice, Rector trains and supervises psychology and psychiatry students, runs workshops nationally and internationally, and is founder and director of the Forest Hill Centre for CBT in Toronto. He has published more than

150 scientific publications and book chapters, and is author of seven books.

Foreword writer **Robert L. Leahy, PhD,** is author or editor of twenty-nine books, including *If Only...: Finding Freedom from Regret, The Worry Cure,* and *The Jealousy Cure.* He is director of the American Institute for Cognitive Therapy in New York, NY, and clinical professor of psychology at Weill Cornell Medical College.

Real change is possible

For more than forty-five years, New Harbinger has published proven-effective self-help books and pioneering workbooks to help readers of all ages and backgrounds improve mental health and well-being, and achieve lasting personal growth. In addition, our spirituality books offer profound guidance for deepening awareness and cultivating healing, self-discovery, and fulfillment.

Founded by psychologist Matthew McKay and Patrick Fanning, New Harbinger is proud to be an independent, employee-owned company. Our books reflect our core values of integrity, innovation, commitment, sustainability, compassion, and trust. Written by leaders in the field and recommended by therapists worldwide, New Harbinger books are practical, accessible, and provide real tools for real change.

newharbingerpublications

MORE BOOKS from
NEW HARBINGER PUBLICATIONS

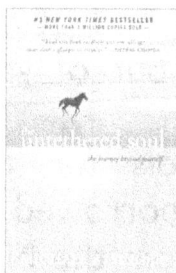

THE UNTETHERED SOUL
The Journey Beyond Yourself

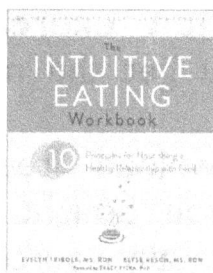

THE INTUITIVE EATING WORKBOOK
Ten Principles for Nourishing a Healthy Relationship with Food

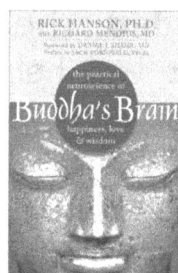

BUDDHA'S BRAIN
The Practical Neuroscience of Happiness, Love, and Wisdom

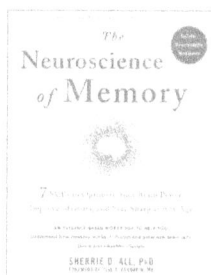

THE NEUROSCIENCE OF MEMORY
Seven Skills to Optimize Your Brain Power, Improve Memory, and Stay Sharp at Any Age

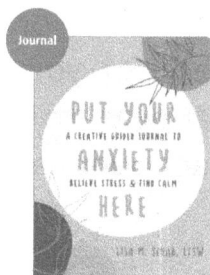

PUT YOUR ANXIETY HERE
A Creative Guided Journal to Relieve Stress and Find Calm

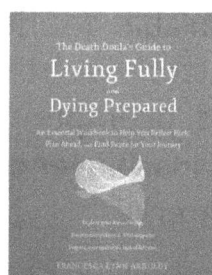

THE DEATH DOULA'S GUIDE TO LIVING FULLY AND DYING PREPARED
An Essential Workbook to Help You Reflect Back, Plan Ahead, and Find Peace on Your Journey

newharbingerpublications
1-800-748-6273 / newharbinger.com
(VISA, MC, AMEX / prices subject to change without notice)
Follow Us

Don't miss out on new books from New Harbinger.
Subscribe to our email list at **newharbinger.com/subscribe**

Did you know there are free tools you can download for this book?

Free tools are things like **worksheets, guided meditation exercises,** and **more** that will help you get the most out of your book.

You can download free tools for this book—whether you bought or borrowed it, in any format, from any source—from the New Harbinger website. All you need is a NewHar binger.com account. Just use the URL provided in this book to view the free tools that are available for it. Then, click on the "download" button for the free tool you want, and follow the prompts that appear to log in to your N ewHarbinger.com account and download the material.

You can also save the free tools for this book to your **Free Tools Library** so you can access them again anytime, just by logging in to your account! Just look for this button on the book's free tools page.

+ Save this to my free tools library

If you need help accessing or downloading free tools, visit **newharbinger.com/faq** or contact us at **customerservice@newharbinger.com.**

Back Cover Material

Redefine the aging process and live life to the fullest!

For even the fittest, healthiest, and most vibrant among us, there are inevitable challenges that come from growing older. Major life events such as retirement, the death of a loved one, physical and emotional changes, and shifting social roles can lead to feelings of fear, uncertainty, loss of control—as well as anxiety and depression. But aging doesn't have to be something that leaves you anxious, sad, or depressed. You *can* carve your own path and take charge of the aging process—*and* your mental well-being.

This workbook offers evidence-based skills drawn from cognitive behavioral therapy (CBT) to help you learn the art of flexible thinking, so you can worry less and feel more engaged with life. You'll discover strategies for managing anxiety and depression, as well as lifestyle tips to help reduce symptoms in the future. If growing older has you feeling anxious, upset, or stressed, this handbook can help you discover a life of greater vitality and joy. **You are worth it!**

"This easy-to-read manual will teach you invaluable skills for improving your

mood, getting back into the swing of life, and achieving your goals."—**JUDITH BECK, PHD,** president of The Beck Institute for Cognitive Behavior Therapy

This empowering guide will help you:
- **Learn the art of flexible thinking**
- **Redefine what it means to age**
- **Improve mental health and increase well-being**
- **Live life to the fullest**

JULIE ERICKSON, PhD, is a clinical psychologist, and adjunct faculty member in the department of applied psychology and human development at the University of Toronto. She maintains an active clinical practice focusing on the treatment of adults across the lifespan.

NEIL A. RECTOR, PhD, is a clinical psychologist, director of the mood and anxiety program in the department of psychiatry at the Sunnybrook Health Sciences Centre, and a full professor at the University of Toronto. In addition to having an active CBT practice, he has published more than 150 scientific publications and book chapters, and is author of seven books.

www.ingramcontent.com/pod-product-compliance
Lightning Source LLC
Chambersburg PA
CBHW010143270326
41928CB00019B/3247